crews

crews

Gang
Members
Talk to
Maria
Hinojosa

photographs by
German Perez

harcourt brace & company
San Diego   New York   London

SMICA

Names of the interviewees have been changed throughout.

Photographs copyright © 1995 by German Perez
The news report on page 152 was originally broadcast on National Public Radio's
"All Things Considered," and was edited by Larry Abramson.

Library of Congress Cataloging-in-Publication Data is available upon request
LC #94-12173
ISBN 0-15-292873-1   ISBN 0-15-200283-9 (pbk)
The text was set in Perpetua and Futura Extra Bold.

Designed by Lisa Peters
Printed in the United States of America
First edition
A B C D E

For our families and our ancestors,

who gave us roots and wings and dreams—

And for all the children who, in the

face of solitude, have looked for family, wherever it may be—

And for all those who "dare to be good"

—M. H. and G. P.

contents

to go dancing?

The news broke in a big way in New York City.

A group of kids mugging a family of out-of-towners. One kid, Brian, defended his mother, and another kid, Rocstar, stabbed him with a knife, killed him, and put the bloody knife back in his pocket. Later reports stated that the kids had wanted the money to go out dancing.

I remember hearing the news back in the fall of 1990. A young man, a tourist from Utah, was visiting New York City, checking out tennis tournaments with his family, when he was stabbed to death on a subway platform. I hadn't even realized they had those tennis tournaments right here in the city. I always thought they were in London or Paris or other places. But the tournament was a big event in lots of people's minds and it was a big deal for Brian Watkins, who was a tennis freak and loved New York City, including the subways. But that night other New York kids were out to do their city thing, too, and it turned out to be a tragedy. Everybody lost something that night. Brian lost his life. The rest of us, kids and adults, lost some of our peace of mind.

The news broke in a big way in New York City. A group of kids mugging a family of out-of-towners. One kid, Brian, defended his mother, and another kid, Rocstar, stabbed him with a knife, killed him, and put the bloody knife back in his pocket. Later reports stated that the kids who mugged the Watkins family, and Rocstar, who killed Brian, had wanted the money to go out dancing.

What??? To go *dancing?* I had a hard time understanding this, just as lots of people did. I kept asking myself—what makes it so easy now for kids to turn to violence? What makes it so easy for a kid to reach in his pocket and pull out a knife and stab someone? Those were the questions I wanted answered when I went out to do my story for National Public Radio (NPR®).

Everybody in the papers and on TV called the kids who killed Brian gang members. But the kids on the street set me straight. It wasn't about gangs. Nobody called them that or thought about them that way, either. They were called *crews*. And in Brooklyn and other places around the city, they were also called *posses*. "There aren't no gangs around here," they said. "We just have our crews." And what's a crew? A bunch of kids who hang out. And like all the bunches of kids who hang out when they're young, there are good ones and bad ones. Hip crews and not-so-hip crews. Crews that just hang and chill together. Other crews that hang out to get paid—make money however they can. But almost every-body's got a crew to catch their back. In the city, they say, you've always got to have someone looking out for your back.

Everybody complains about teenagers and the bad things they do. But teenagers will always test their limits. Who sits down and talks to them? Who asks what they feel and why? Who wants to listen, no matter how painful the answers might be?

I wanted to listen.

And I wanted to know why.

The radio report as it aired nationally on NPR® November 6, 1990, appears in this book. After the story ran, I got lots of nasty letters. "How could you give airtime to these street kids?" people wrote. "They don't deserve anything."

A lot of people appreciated the story, too. It won lots of awards. A few weeks after the story ran on the radio, an editor called me and asked me to write a book. But I was scared. I had never written a book before and didn't know too many people who had. Anyway, this person came and visited me. She told me again that I should write this book. We went out to lunch, and she told me a story about a friend of hers who had been killed violently. We need to hear these stories, she said. We need to hear from kids. And you can talk to them, she said. I knew then I should write this book. A book of stories from the powerless, in their own voices, in their own words. *CREWS.*

About a week after Brian Watkins was killed I went out to Flushing to find and interview members of Rocstar's crew, FTS (Flushing's Top Society). The media had zeroed in on Flushing, a middle-class neighborhood where people from all over the world lived together. The kids were giddy with all the cameras and microphones; it was their chance to be in the limelight. But lots of the kids who talked to the TV and newspapers didn't even know who the members of FTS were. By the time I got to Flushing, several days after the murder, most reporters had left the story behind, the kids who were anxious for attention had gotten their fill of it, and Flushing had been labeled the gang capital of New York City. Nothing could have been further from the truth.

It wasn't about gangs in Flushing, but it was about crews. Crews, I was to find out, are everywhere.

I took the number seven subway all the way to the end of the line. I made my way over to the park where FTS hung out just after school. First I met some young girls. They must have been twelve or thirteen. They talked eagerly about the guys from FTS, maybe because they were flattered that I would even think they knew anything about them. Then I talked to some boys of about the same age. They talked as if they knew everything about everybody in the neighborhood, and they started copping an attitude with me. But then I saw a person walking toward me with a group of older kids. It was Coki. He was seventeen at the time and was wearing his hoodie way up over his head, shadowing his eyes. He was smoking Newports. He talked real tough, cutting people off, kind of loud and curt. When he talked, everybody listened. The younger kids kind of backed away. It was clear Coki did have ties to FTS. But I had been expecting something a little different. When Coki pulled down his hoodie I saw the peach fuzz over his lips. He had a little smirk, like a cartoon character's, and eyes that bounced all over. He smiled a lot.

Our first conversation took place in 1990, as we leaned against some cars outside a junior high school. After a while, the principal of the school asked us to move off school property. We stepped down a few yards and talked under the shade of a tree while mothers with little kids in strollers walked by, oblivious to our conversation about the history of crews right there in their own neighborhood.

coki: This here is original FTS. It all started out in this school right here. We were HBO, Homeboys Only. We got into the crews 'cause you gotta have respect, 'cause if you don't have respect— Let's put it this way, if you don't have respect on the street then you gonna get picked on, always. If you're not gonna get robbed on the street then you gonna get hit on the street, if not that, then someone is gonna do something to you, so you can't let that happen. So after we were HBO then it turned into FTS—Flushing's Top Society—Fight To Survive. But FTS was more like a go-out, hang-out kind of group. That's what it was about. But it wasn't about no violence. I mean, once in a while, you do have to defend yourself, that's true. What happened was wrong, but I know that Rocstar didn't mean to kill him.

mh: This is a pretty nice neighborhood. It's better than the neighborhood I live in—

coki: Put it this way. It's not the kind of neighborhood that you bring up your kids in anymore. I mean, when I first came to this neighborhood, this neighborhood was nice. You could walk down the streets and nothing happened. Now you walk down the street late at night, and you walking by yourself, and if you are packing or with one or two of your boys then nothing is gonna happen to you, but if you by yourself, chances are that you'll get rushed, you'll get robbed, something will happen to you. Chances are. I'm not saying it happens every day but it happens a lot.

mh: Is that why there are more and more crews coming up?

coki: Right now the reason more and more crews are coming up is because people are starting to see that Flushing is becoming bad and somebody has to take control. Somebody wants to be on top. And the people who got on top all be running Flushing, let's put it that way. Right now what's running Flushing, what's always run Flushing back since the 1970s —I got friends who got clippings of this from twenty years ago—it's 20 Park. That's the number-one crew no matter what. But I'm also a member of FTS. Right now I am what is known as an intelligent hood. I mean, I go to school. I dropped out of school, then I realized a lot of things. I went back. I want my diploma. It's gonna mean something to me. I'm gonna need it in the future. But right now if somebody wants to take control over here or whatever, they can't touch us. They can't touch us 'cause we got the name, you know what I mean? But we ain't gonna stop them either. We ain't gonna stop nobody from running the streets—as long as they don't mess with us, we ain't gonna mess with them. I should go home and bring you my medallion that I used to have. You seen those black African medallions? We didn't have no Africa on them 'cause we ain't from Africa. But ours has CD on the top and on the bottom it has FTS, and we had a bullet in the middle. Here it's different than in L.A. We don't fight over colors. We fight over territory.

mh: There are people who will say that you kids don't really need anything. You guys are all right. Your parents are working. You have an OK neighborhood. You're going to school and stuff. So people will ask themselves, Why do they have to be so violent?

coki: It's like this. You gotta protect what's yours. You gotta protect your neighborhood. Put it this way. Usually when people come from another neighborhood into your neighborhood, it's to start trouble. Take that from me and take that from everyone here. Put it like this. Would you like somebody coming into your house, taking what's yours, laying back in your couch like it's theirs or whatever? You don't like that, right? OK, this is the same thing. This is my house. I could lay in my streets. I was raised here. I wasn't born here. I'm an Ecuadorian citizen but I was raised here. And I mean I don't like no one coming into my neighborhood doing whatever they want 'cause they give my neighborhood a bad name. We have conflicts.

mh: What do you fight with?

coki: Fistfights, with bats, anything you could get your hands on. You're an adult, right? I am seventeen years old. I am pretty sure, almost definitely sure, that I have lived twice as much as you have—through twice as many things as you have. I've been through everything. So you can't give me a lecture 'cause I already know wassup. I mean, you might be able to lecture me in certain things, but in most things, naw. Forget about it.

mh: People are saying that in FTS and the other crews, one of the things you needed to do to be a member was to have an initiation.

coki: The other crews before didn't do nothing. We were the only crew that gave initiations, FTS. And the initiation wasn't about robbing or mugging no one. The initiation was to have ten or fifteen of us, and you make a circle and you just throw punches. You throw punches. You aren't supposed to land one in the face,

but if you did, what the hell? There are fifteen guys. You don't
know who hit you. The other rule is that you can't hit in the
testicles. No one would ever kick you like that. You just have to
fight against fifteen guys. And we gave a lot of guys initiations. One
of the guys that's in jail with Rocstar we initiated, me and my boys
from 20 Park. It's like a mini–bum rush. I've always represented
20 Park first, then FTS.

mh: Let's say a woman was walking down the street, would you
guys say, "Let's go rob her?"

coki: Naw. Remember what I told you. I am an intelligent hoodlum. I'm intelligent. This is what happens. You need money for
the weekend, that's all. We need more paying jobs for us out here.
Let me tell you something. I went applying for a job about a month
ago. I went looking for a job two days in a row. Two or three days
in a row. I applied in every store that I could. I never got called. I
took off my hat and went like a gentleman; I asked nicely. I asked
like a civilized man, and what am I supposed to do if I can't get
money? If they had more jobs for teenagers, we wouldn't be out
here hanging out. We would be working.

mh: It's true that jobs are hard to come by, but why do you
do this other stuff? Thirty years ago your father would not have
said, "Let's go get paid by whatever means possible." What has
happened?

coki: The difference between now and thirty years ago, times
are hard now, believe me, times are hard. Put it like this. If you got

no bread on your table and your parents can't hack it, you gotta do something about it. That's your family. That comes first. So if you got no money for your bread on your table you gotta go look for it. You gotta look for money somehow. If there's no job you gotta get paid somehow. Right or wrong. Put it like this. You gotta kill to survive. That's how it's getting. I know it's bad but times are getting hard out here. Believe me. After a while when you hang out on the streets and you see you ain't doing nothing, you see you ain't going anywhere, either you turn into the bad or, you are brave enough, you go for the good. If you are brave enough you stick it out through school. 'Cause school is not fun. It is boring. But if you realize that you ain't doing nothing here at all then you might as well go for something good. You see you have a future. Look, there's one thing. You must never ever forget where you come from. 'Cause if you forget where you come from you have no morals and no respect for yourself. But these days there are people out who have guns. Everybody has guns! In every neighborhood! And they get guns and we get guns and they try to do this or that, and we ain't gonna let them! We ain't gonna have it. We can't. I mean, I was raised here. These are my streets! I can lay down over here and go, Ahhhh! And I want to feel comfortable when I lay down. And—it's just gonna get worse. There's gonna be a lot of fighting here. It sucks to walk down the street and have to have one eye behind your head and you thinking, When is that knife coming in? When am I gonna get shot? In a way it's scary, but in another way, you just don't care no more. If it's gonna happen, it's gonna happen.

mh: Do you think that's what Rocstar is feeling? That it just had to happen?

coki: Like I said, Rocstar did not mean to kill that kid! I know he didn't mean to kill that kid! It's not fair! Whatever happened happened. I mean, it's not right that the kid got killed first of all, but it's not right that the man is gonna spend twenty-five years to life in jail for something that he didn't mean to do. I don't know if he did it or not. I wasn't there. But for something he didn't mean to do, that's not fair. Just the way that it's not fair that the kid died, but I mean, the kid is dead, he's dead, what can you do? You can't bring him back to life by putting a man in jail for twenty-five years. I mean, the least they can do is drop some charges. Give him the robbery charge, OK, but drop the murder. I know the guy. I was raised with him and I know what he's about. He's not about murdering.

mh: Is it worth it? Is this violence worth it?

coki: Like I said, it's worth it when you were raised here. It's worth it when you can walk down your street and feel safe, when you know that you're so bad that you're walking down the street, and there's other bad dudes out there and they can't touch you. That's when it's worth it.

Our next meeting was set up for me to go and do a tagging

session with FTS. I got to the park around 7:00 P.M. I stood on that corner waiting for Coki for about an hour and a half.

I was about to leave when I saw a group of kids walking toward me. They were acting kind of wild, jumping up and down, letting out hoots and hollers. Coki walked to the corner and started high-fiving with his friends. He was dissing me in no uncertain terms. Then Shank came up to me. The rest of the crew kept acting crazy. Shank looked young but had a serious tone whenever he spoke to me. He had almond-shaped eyes and dark eyebrows, which some-times gave him a devilish look.

mh: So what happened? Where were you guys? Why were you late?

shank: We went to jail for assault. I mean, they were identify-ing us for assault, that's all. It was like a gang sweep; the detective car just passed by, and they sent us to the precinct and gave us a number, and we stood against the wall, and then we were supposed to get picked out if we did the assault, but luckily the guy didn't see who did it so we got off scot-free.

mh: Does that mean that you did it?

shank: Yeah. I mean, we're telling the truth right here so I'll tell you the truth. Last Friday we were hanging out. We saw victim-looking people and we just did it and that's it. I get my anger out doing stuff like that.

mh: What do you mean you get your anger out?

shank: I know it sounds kind of insane or irrational, but during the week, I'm in school and I have to do good 'cause I'm planning to go into the Marine Corps. I have to pass since it's senior year. So I gotta stay in school, and meanwhile my friends are telling me to cut out and I'm like, no, no, no, so I hold like little pieces of anger. They all add up to the weekend when I get to do what I really want. Maybe I don't have money, I don't work, so maybe I see a kid who looks like he has money so I go by myself and do him. And with that money we probably hang out, go to the movies, or whatever. It's not hard to identify a vic. You see a person that looks like he has money, he dresses nice and stuff. You can just see that he has money. It's easy to tell. 'Cause I don't have money and I just look at myself, and if he looks better than me then he must have money. Then we just try. If we're not lucky then he just gets beat up for no reason, but if we are then we get money.

mh: Do you consider yourself a violent person?

shank: I don't know. I get swings. It's not under my control 'cause, believe me, I've tried so hard to control it. But it's like I can't give it up. It's a combination of peer pressure and like having to release something, and this is how you release it. By doing this.

mh: Can you think of another way that you might be able to release it?

shank: I've tried, believe me, I've tried. I've tried art, I've tried . . . how do you say . . . um, constructive things, but I don't know. It just don't give me the same feeling of release.

mh: What exactly do you feel?

shank: I feel like, aaahhhhhh. Like letting out a deep breath. That's the only thing I can do to express it. Aaaahhh. It's like a risk I have to take and, I don't know, I love it. It's risk, you know, like why people do stunts and stuff, 'cause of the feeling, the euphoria you get out of it.

mh: So why should I feel safe around you guys?

shank: You come up to us, that's all. We hate people who are scared of us. You know, pussies. We hate people who are like, "Get away from us" and stuff. If you have the initiative and the courage to come up to us, we give you respect right there 'cause not everybody does that. I mean, we have respect for you. You're older. You're a mature woman. And you asked us! That's all people have to do. Like if people want to hang out with us, just approach us.

mh: So if you see someone who's scared of you, it makes it easier to want to attack them?

shank: Yeah, yeah.

mh: Is it a race thing?

shank: Naw, not at all. We have a lot of friends who hang out who are white. But right now, it's, like, we're the minorities and we have to prove to people, to whoever is on top now, that we could achieve and stuff. Even if it's, like, on the violent side, it's still the same concept to me. Like if I went over you, at least I went over you at something. It might be a stupid thing, but at least I win over you at something. I know it sounds dumb. Believe me, I know. But what else can you do? Maybe it's when you're brought up in this kind of environment. As soon as I came here, I went in a crew, just like that. At least it's not like in Los Angeles. Over there we could be talking right here and people drive by and, pop, pop, you get shot; they feel good—that gives them their release of frustration. Right here, we just do it with our hands.

mh: What's the frustration?

shank: Anything. Any simple thing. If I try to better myself in any way, people just look at me and say, "What are you doing? You ain't supposed to be like that. You're supposed to be a hoodlum." If I try to go up an inch the pressure drops down a foot. So it's hard to deal with that. You go up one step and go back two. I guess it starts at home with your parents. Even though they don't mean it, they put you down with not appreciating what you do for them or what you do for yourself, which is doing good in school. With the police department, and excuse me if I say it, but most of the white police department has problems with us. Like one day I was walking to my grandmother's house and the cops came up to me and said, "Get the hell outta here." And I was just going to my grandma's house. Maybe there were some guys messing around before, but I was just going to my grandma's house. And they were like, "Yo, walk the other way." And I said, "I have to go to my grandmother's house." They said, "That's a bad excuse. Leave." I just went around the block. Some teachers do the same stuff.

People who are supposed to be there to help you. But instead of helping you, they're there to kick you in the face while you're try- ing to climb up the ladder.

Like I said, my answer to all of this frustration is to do what I do. And I feel good, I can't deny it. I wish I could change it 'cause I know it's bad. Sometimes I feel like I shouldn't be doing this, 'cause I was brought up by my grandmother. She brought me up strictly Catholic, through the Church, and I say, God, please help me, but he can't. There's no other way for me to relieve the frustration. Or no other way suitable for me.

shank

the street is alive

It's easy to hurt and easy to do bad things. It's

the easiest way out. I'm gonna beat everyone

up and that's how I am gonna get respect. But

it's not easy to say to someone that you want to

work in their company. It's easier to be bad.

Six months after my first interview with

Shank, I won an award for my radio piece

on the crews. I called Shank and asked

him if he would like to join me at the

awards ceremony. He said yes. The awards

night was a gala event at a luxury hotel

in midtown Manhattan. Women wore

shimmering dresses and the men had on tuxedos. Shank was a little self-conscious; he had a hard time looking people straight in the eye. He picked at his gourmet meal, twitching in the new shirt and tie he had bought for the event.

I asked him if he would join me at the podium when I was called up to receive the award. His eyes popped open, and he almost lost his breath when I told him I thought it would be great if he got up there and talked to a room full of journalists, just the way he had spoken to me when we first met. He looked nervous.

When they announced my award, I stood up to go to the podium. Shank hesitated, and then, as if he were daring himself to do it, stood up and followed me. I spoke briefly about the power of the media to affect people's lives, to give voice to the voiceless. Then I introduced Shank and handed the microphone over to him. He took a deep breath and told the crowd of over one thousand that his life had been transformed after he had been interviewed. He said that as he heard himself talking about the things he had done he realized how wrong they were. He realized he wanted to change. He said no one had ever asked him about his life. No one had ever listened to what he had to say. No one had ever told him he was intelligent. After the interview, he had started to believe in himself.

The crowd gave Shank a standing ovation. People cheered and applauded. He was a star that night. They came over to shake his hand and take his photograph. But after the party, the click-click and the bright lights of the camera flashes were gone. Shank went home, back to the street, to his crew, where the one thing he was known for was his ability to knock someone out with one punch. There it didn't matter that Shank had a way with words or that he had dreams about being good.

Two years after that magical night, Shank and I met again to talk about his life and the crews of Queens.

shank: I came here from Colombia when I was twelve. By the time I was thirteen, I was with Chinese gangs 'cause I look a little Chinese. I used to love to play in arcades, video games. So my aunt took me to a spot called Entertainment World. There were funny smells, the music thumping and the lights in my eyes. . . . All the people, they looked happy. But then the summer came and in the summer . . . I was all alone, I didn't have any friends. I memorized how to get to Coney Island, where there were more arcades. I wanted to go every day. So out of my naïveté, I started recycling cans since my family drank a lot of soda. And then I became like a bag boy. I started picking up cans from the street, and I thought it was all right, I didn't think it was bad. But then I realized that maybe I looked

homeless, and so I stopped doing it because I realized people were looking at me! Like the kids were mumbling words and laughing. Even though I didn't understand what they were saying, I could tell they were making fun of me and laughing at me. I guess that was when people's opinions started mattering to me. I knew a little English, and once a guy came up to me and said, "You want five dollars?" And I was like, "Yeah!" And then he said, "Come with me. I need you to do me a favor." So I went with him and we started walking far away and then into an alley, and I said, "What are you talking about? What favor?" And then he said, "Just stand there. I want you to do me a sexual favor." And I ran and I remember thinking, Damn, I almost got burned—that this wasn't a movie, it was real. Something could happen to me. And I ran away all the way to the train and I never went there again. I was scared 'cause I suddenly woke up and realized I didn't have anyone, no family, and I was far away. I took it as a Wake up! kind of sign. I relieved all the blame from the guy that tried to do that to me and put all the blame on myself for being so naive. So I just went back to going to Entertainment World, with a few quarters from the cans. And I used to hang out there a lot. It wasn't just the video games that I liked. It was all the people around and the electronic noises, and I guess . . . the company. I had no friends, but I had all the kids around me and that was good enough. There was this Chinese guy who always had two guys standing by his sides as he played, and I looked at the video screen and it was registering a lot of credit, like if he was putting in a lot of quarters, but he wasn't. And I just kept looking at him until I saw that he had a key to open the machine. And he also used to steal the money. His two friends were his blockers to protect him. One day he told me to stand there and I did, and then he let me play and gave me some quarters. And then we became friends. His name was Gin and there was Chow and Lin; that was the immediate crew. They spoke Cantonese and had thick accents in English. So I used to block him and get my share of the loot, and then I didn't have to pick up cans anymore. And as we became closer they gave me more money, up to the point that I got my own key. That was the top. It was the master key to open all the games anywhere. So now I had my own key and I could hire my own blockers, and I had a little power—I liked it. I used to go to Lin's house and we used to play Nintendo, and I met a whole bunch of his Chinese friends. The reason my friendship ended with Lin was because one day an older friend of his came to his house. He was talking Chinese and looking at me bad and then he took out a gun. I had seen guns in the movies so I wasn't all impressed. I didn't take it for what it was. I said, "Oh! A gun! I'm gonna tell the cops!" I was joking, but they all got quiet. Then he put the gun to my head and said, "What you gonna tell the cops?" and I got all scared and told him not to shoot and covered my head. He put the gun down and his friend talked him into putting it away. I don't know who he was. But I left the house and never saw those guys again.

————————

The loneliness in Shank's life was overwhelming. He was lonely at home, where his mother barely paid any attention to him. And he was lonely in the new world of New York City. So for two years, Shank concentrated on school and he learned English. He was a good student, his grades averaging in the nineties. Even that, he says, didn't bring much praise from his mother.

In school, Shank was called a hick and a nerd, but he didn't yet realize he was being made fun of. He couldn't understand why other kids slapped him or tripped him in the school hallways. Inside, Shank's loneliness was finding a new partner—anger.

Shank met the guys from the 20 Park crew through a girl who liked him. She liked him because he was so quiet. In the first few weeks of hanging out with the guys, Shank said very little. "I was just a cheerleader for them. Whatever they said, I would just say, 'Yeah, yeah, yeah.'"

The first night the crew took Shank to hang out, they smoked weed, drank Southern Comfort, jumped a subway turnstile, and beat up an innocent bystander, a vic. In the craziness of that first night Shank kicked the person in the head while his crew beat him up. "It was like euphoria," he says. "It was like I was possessed and did something I really didn't want to and had no reason to."

Shank was down with 20 Park. And that gave him connections with another crew, on the street where his new friend Coki lived.

————————

shank: I was a new person. I wasn't the Shank that came from Colombia that was a nice kid. All of that was put in a closet or maybe outrun by the new me. I forgot about a lot of things. I forgot about who I used to be. When I lived with my grandma back in Colombia, I knew my time to be home. I was *educado* by my grandparents. But in New York City my mom didn't care what time I came home. At first when I started hanging out, I was careful about the time I would come home, 'cause I felt like I needed to be home, that I had a time to be home. Once by mistake I fell asleep at my friend's house and I thought, Oh no! Mom is gonna kill me. Thinking she was gonna treat me the same way my grandmother would. So I went home and they were all asleep. I woke up the next morning thinking they were gonna scream at me and nothing happened. The next coupla times I was late I called home to say I was sorry I was coming home late and they were like, "Don't worry about it." It wasn't that I was thinking that they didn't care but instead that I had freedom. I could hang out more. I had no more strings.

mh: And school?

shank: Tenth grade I managed to pass, but around that time is when FTS showed up. I became a member of FTS. I was the first one to go through the initiation process. I got initiated the roughest 'cause I had to fight the roughest guy from FTS. His name was Touch, a black guy who was real muscular. I had to fight him one-on-one, but he was like an elder and I didn't want to hit him. He caught me on the side of the head and I got dizzy so they stopped it. But I wasn't satisfied. So I said I wanted to go in the circle, and everybody that was down with FTS formed a circle around me and I had to fight my way out. They put you in a circle and everybody starts hitting you . . . your own friends. And that affects your mind. Seeing your own friends hitting you. It hurts. It hurts your heart. You rejudge things. It makes you feel bad, like you can't be totally friends, and it puts you in a spot where you can't even trust your own friends. Anybody in a gang or a crew will tell you they don't trust nobody. Respect is another thing, but trust—nobody trusts nobody. Nobody.

Anger is Shank's best friend. Anger is always with him and whenever he needs it, it is there. It never failed him and never let him down. For Shank, anger isn't an inexplicable emotion that comes and goes. It has been with Shank from the time he was a small kid, more constantly than any human being.

This chapter is hard to read, and it was hard for Shank to talk about. But on the street, you carry your marks of violence like other kids carry their trophies from swimming, diving, and basketball.

shank: I was thinking today, no matter what you do in this life, somebody is always gonna be against you. I was thinking that no matter where you go in this world you ain't gonna find peace until you die. And I was thinking today how I tried to get out, but I can't stop the way I am and become whatever it is that I want to be unless everybody goes along with that change, too, or at least everybody I know that has been a part of my life from when these changes started happening in me. And I guess that's why I am trying to get my friends to change too.

mh: 'Cause that would make it easier for you to change.

shank: Yeah. And I realize that is the only way it's gonna happen, and since no one is cooperating then I am just gonna have to remain like this.

mh: Is it really anger that you have inside of you, Shank?

shank: I don't know. That's the closest explanation. I feel pressure. Like something real dense here, in the center of my chest. I even feel like I am gonna lose my breath when I talk about it. It's like it wants to get out. Whatever is holding it back—my conscience—is like a door and that stuff inside is slamming against it—like pop, pop, pop. Yet my conscience . . . or whatever it is . . . my good judgment's strength is not infinite. That's how I feel. I feel tired, exhausted of holding it back.

mh: In your mind and memory and your heart and soul, when you think about what has happened in the past, is there something that you did with your own two hands that was the thing you feel worst about?

shank: [He kind of groans and mumbles.] I never felt bad. I never shot nobody. I am scared of guns, I think it's unfair to die for a gun. I consider myself a warrior and if you're gonna fight, you give the person a chance to defend themselves and there is no way to defend yourself against a gun. So I never believed in them. I felt the power that comes from them. Once you have a gun you feel like you are on the top of the world. But I've never used one. I've used knives and my hands most of the time. But once, three guys had a plan to rob a drugstore, a big drugstore. So we went there—

mh: How did you figure out your plan? You three guys sat around a table or what?

shank: One of the guys involved in the robbery used to work there so he knew everything about it. He knew who was gonna be there and where the money was. Who was the security, how many cashiers there would be, what would be the best time . . . But it

wasn't an inside job 'cause he wasn't working there anymore. So there were three of us. One was the driver and two were the guys to go in. I was one to go in. So I went in with my friend, and we see the little office where the cashiers go to count their money, and the plan was for me to go in there and even though I never shot nobody, I used a gun that time, to intimidate the people. So I went in there with a gun—

mh: What kind of a gun?

shank: A .357 Magnum. A snub nose.

mh: That's a machine gun?

shank: No, my friend had a machine gun. A submachine gun. A Mac 10. So my friend was there and we looked around. We checked out one security guard, a coupla cashiers, and I thought we weren't gonna do it. We were real scared. We felt like all eyes were on us, but then out of the blue, I just got quiet. I just didn't care anymore, and I just went into the little office and pulled out the gun and there were cashiers counting their money 'cause the store was about to close so they were all there . . . And I said, "All of you get on the floor—or I'm gonna blow your head off!" And I told one girl to get on the speaker and call the manager to come to the booth. So she did that. So the manager came and I pulled him in. And I pulled the hammer. I cocked the gun and I told him that my friend was out there, that he should empty the money from the booth and then empty the safe outside the office and give him all of the money. And I said, "If you try anything I'm gonna shoot one of the cashiers." So he was like, OK, OK. He got the money and then he came back in and said my friend had all the money. I had a blade so I cut all the telephone cords while the cashiers were lying down. They were scared and had their hands like in a praying position, which is the moral of the story I get to later on. They were all scared and trembling. I was about to leave, but before I did I said to the cashiers, "Stay here and don't make any moves or else your boss is gonna get it now." And I walked with him. And my friend was pushing a shopping cart full of money. There were a lot of singles. Lots of boxes and coins. By this time it was obvious what was going on so security came to approach us and my friend and I just took out our weapons and said, "Everybody run to the back of the store NOW!" And the security ran to the back, too. So we went out, put the stuff in the car, and that's it. We went to another friend's house and divided the money, went home, changed clothes and came back out and started drinking beers and doing the same stuff like before.

mh: And what is the moral of the story?

shank: That is the most important part. The reason why I think that is the worst thing I ever did. It's because of the girls, they really got to me, they were so young, maybe eighteen or so. They were whimpering. I had never seen somebody so scared and in my mind I was like, Don't worry, girls, I'm not gonna shoot you! I even would have told them 'cause that's how strongly I felt about it. Just tell them not to worry, just play cool, I wanted to be friendly with them, be sympathetic . . . But, no. Now I was some-body to really be afraid of and they were terrified. And it hit me. I was thinking about it for two weeks. They thought they were gonna die. That's so messed up. I left a mark in their heads, like for a long time. Maybe now they are paranoid, maybe now they are scared to go into drugstores, or be out late at night. . . . And I really hate people who are afraid of me. Not hate them, but really dislike the fact that sometimes people have been apprehensive of me. And that day, forget it, everybody was like crying and trembling. . . . The same way I used to be when I was little and my father would come home drunk and smacking my mom. And that impression I got from seeing those people made me say, "That's enough!" That's when I made my decision about which road to take. 'Cause it was too much psychologically, emotionally. I just couldn't handle that. It was like, ugh, this is what I am becoming. And I don't want to be like this. . . . You know, inflicting so much fear in a person. And although my father meant to be like that towards my mom, keep her scared and stuff, I didn't want to be like that. I just did it for the money and money made me forget. I bought a lot of things. And my mom used to say, "Where did you get your money?" and I would just say nothing. I just gave her like a thousand dollars and told her to put it in the bank. She used to ask, but she never really cared where it came from.

mh: When you went home and changed your clothes, what was going on inside? Was it that you were rich or feeling bad?

shank: My mind was fluctuating through three different things to think about. One was those girls, the middle one was the money, and the third one was looking at myself. I saw that power in me when I did what I wanted. I made things happen when I wanted them to. I was just surprised that from inside of me came this energy that just did what I had to do. And that feeling is magnified by me having gotten away with it. 'Cause maybe if I hadn't gotten away with it I would be calling myself a dummy. But I was on top. It was that no matter what, I was gonna get what I wanted. Whether people complied or not didn't matter. I was gonna get my way and I did. And I did because of me. I had a one-track mind. Once I set my eyes on something that's all I thought about. I didn't see the consequences of it and that is ignorance. 'Cause if I was thinking about all that then I wouldn't have done it, definitely. 'Cause I could have even gotten my friends in trouble. But I was thinking about the money and how I would enjoy it. That outweighed the other side. It made me forget about the family and other stuff. And that made me think, too. The last thing I want to do is hurt people and that night I hurt those girls emotionally. And when I first got arrested and spent a little time in Rikers, I hurt my family. It's not the time. I could have been there one day or one year, but it's the same, 'cause they are gonna be like, "What did we do wrong?"

mh: You did this after you had been in Rikers? And even after being in Rikers, in jail—

shank: Yeah, I had been in Rikers once before, when I got arrested for carrying a gun that wasn't even mine. That was more than a year before this thing happened. But being in jail makes you a worse criminal. I learned so many things in that short period of time. I spent eight days in Rikers Island and I learned a lot of things about crime. How to go about doing stuff, how to set up your little drug ring, where to go to get stuff, how to do things . . . I was scared in the beginning. There are always people looking to see what they could get from you, but the talk of the town over there is how to do crime. It's not like, Damn, as soon as I get out I am gonna get my life straight. No, everybody is just talking about when they get out they will resume their things and not make the same mistakes that got them caught.

mh: Were you scared when you were in the drugstore?

shank: I was scared. But I couldn't back out. I guess it was pride. I didn't want to look bad. Which is dumb. I didn't want to look like a half-stepper. . . . I had done too much of that in my life before. Set my mind to do something and then just said forget it. So that time it was like that wasn't gonna happen. Enough of that. I always felt like I went halfway. I didn't fulfill what I wanted to do. Like with school I was messing up and I wanted to do better and then the teachers start messing with you, saying, oh no, you can't be good enough for this and smart enough for that. And you know how smart you are. I knew how smart I was. In eleventh grade around all this time, I tried to do good in school and they look at your grades and say bullshit. And instead of believing in yourself and how smart you know you are, you give up. You give them the power to decide about your life. But now it's hard. I think about how many of the people I hurt were fathers or big brothers. That all affects me now. I am more conscious of what I do. 'Cause everything is all tied together. Every action has a reaction. And if I do good, maybe I get good reactions. But if I do bad, if it doesn't happen to me the bad comes around to someone else. Even my little brother. I used to see that he looks up to me. And I was like, Damn, I need to change. I used to come home drunk and he would tell me in the morning. I would lie and say no, I wasn't drinking, I was tired. But little kids aren't naive. They know what's up. And that's when I realized I had to change, 'cause the last thing I want is for my brother to go through what I am going through. If anything I want to be there to tell him what it's like on the other side. That it's not worth it. But the only way I can do that is if I become a good person. If I tell him don't drink and then I come home drunk—

mh: Where do you think all of this violence comes from? You weren't born violent.

shank: It's easy to hurt and easy

to do bad things. That is the easiest thing to do. It's the easiest way out. It's harder and takes more effort to be good. And a lot of time young people especially see it as a way to be. I'm gonna beat everyone up and that's how I am gonna get respect. Rather than go to school and finish my studies and get a good job, things that take more effort. They want it right there and then. They can get respect by beating someone up or selling drugs or robbing people. It's a lack of patience and too much opportunity to be bad. You go around the street and there is stuff there. Back as a kid in Coney Island, people were offering me to take drugs and even sell drugs. I didn't know what it was about. I used to think selling weed was so bad, but now it's so easy to tell someone to give you some to sell. But it's not easy to say to someone that you want to work in their company. It's easier to be bad.

On the subway on the way to interview Shank one day, I was reading a book about gang-bangers in Los Angeles. By the time I got to Shank's house I was feeling sick. In this book, kids talked about all of the horrible things they had seen in their lives. Some talked about the horrible things they had done. I was still trying to figure out an answer to my original question: How could human beings, young people in particular, be so detached that other people's suffering meant so little to them? In the book I was reading, one kid talks about watching somebody's brains spilling out of their head and how it looked like oatmeal. When I showed that part of the book to Shank, he just laughed. I couldn't believe it.

mh: You think it's funny that the guy says that the brain of some-body who just died looks like oatmeal?

shank: Yeah.

mh: Why?

shank: Thinking of food and thinking of someone's brains. It looks like what the guy was saying in the book. It depends. 'Cause execution style, *se le sale como agua.*

mh: Did you see someone shot execution style?

[Silence]

mh: You don't want to talk about it?

shank: Right now it's that my mind is very analytical. . . . That's going back in time.

mh: You don't want to go back . . .

shank: [Silence] I understand when he was talking about it like that in the book. That's why I thought it was funny. Superficially, if you are just talking about it, it's funny. But when you remember and stuff, then it starts to bother you. I remember all about having the guard up, the guard that protects you from feeling anything. You can't let things like that get to you. That's like feeling pity. Pity comes from seeing someone in a bad spot, and what's a worse spot than getting shot in the head? I saw that happen once when I was little in Colombia, with my father. I just remember driving around in a car and I was in the backseat and my father and the driver were in the front seat and there were two guys next to me. They were all drunk. Ninety percent of the memories I have of my father were of him being drunk. My father showed me a gun that time. I just remember a big black thing.

mh: How old were you?

shank: I don't remember. Maybe four or five. My father gave me the gun and told me to shoot things out the window. I couldn't 'cause it was too heavy. I couldn't pull the trigger. The gun looked real big in my hands so I figure I was real young, with little hands. And I just couldn't shoot. And then we stopped and my father and his friends got out of the car. Then I don't know what happened, but they flipped on one of the guys. To flip is to—it's not like betray—but more like a modern Judas move, but you do it yourself. Like if I am gonna flip on you, all this time we've been friends and then right now I just reverse my actions. So that's what happened with my father's friend and he got shot in the head. I saw the guy standing to my right, and the shooter was to the left and they were talking loud. And the guy was fine and then they just shot him. And he fell.

mh: Do you remember crying then?

shank: No! That is like a flash I remember from my youth. I can tell you that that was before I understood about people dying and stuff. So I wasn't scared. You can't be scared of something you don't understand. But I do remember when I was little I used to get real scared of loud voices and stuff 'cause of the fights my mother had with my father, screaming and all that. Even when I came here, loud noises used to make me tremble 'cause that's how scared I got back then.

mh: Why were you so scared?

shank: My father . . . I couldn't understand that he would come home all nice and treat me like a good son. And other days he used to be completely different. He was flipping. He used to beat up my mom. My mom used to cry and scream, "Aaahhh, aaahhh" . . . and you are confused. I never could understand why he would do that. Until I was older and made the connection that he acted like that 'cause he drank. It's like I am nice to you one day and then the next day, "AAAARRRGGGHHH! What the hell are you doing?" And you think, He is just playing. But then he is not playing. He is being mean and maybe I guess sometimes he did hit me. But I was young. I remember he used to carry me sometimes when he was drunk and then he would just drop me.

I remember once he was carrying me and he just dropped me and I fell hard. He just dropped me. It's like pictures in my mind. I remember one time I was in the patio in my house and I was screwing with the tiles on the floor. And I loosened one of the tiles and then my father came and he hit me with an iron on my knee. And I just remember looking at it and it was bleeding. And I was crying and just looking at the blood. I remember a lot of the connection of the violence with him drinking. Then my grand-mother was always telling me to write to my father, but I haven't done it for six years. The reason why is because six years ago, after I had been writing all of these letters he told me once not to write him with such frequency "because we don't have stuff to talk about if you write me every week." And that was it. I never wrote him back again.

I just remember being so confused and not being able to speak. Just *aguantando* parties around me and loud music, and when I tried to sleep I couldn't. If not loud music, then screaming or something happening, and the only times I got to rest was when I was alone because maybe my mom left and my father did, too. They used to leave me alone. Completely alone. And then my mom got separated from my dad and he moved away, and I used to be left alone because my mother used to go to parties. I used to fight with her, I used to pull her hair and try to block the door for her not to leave me. But she would leave. And I used to be crying all night. Until one night, my grandparents came and took me upstairs to where they used to live and that was it. I stayed there for the rest of the time. I didn't live with her again until I came here to New York City. . . . It's like me and her, we just don't talk. Never! I come here to my house and say hi to her, but there is no connection. I know she is my mom and I care for her, but there is no connection. I always try to understand why that is, but me and her don't talk.

mh: So you've never sat down and tried to talk to her about all of this stuff?

shank: I can't. It's not even about courage. I just don't feel like it. It's just that I have come so far in my life like this that it doesn't matter. She is my mom, but I have never really had parents.

mh: Before you and I talked about any of this stuff, did you talk to anybody about it?

shank: No. I don't know what it is with me. Maybe the human mind has a self-defense system. It tries to erase that which hurts you a lot. I remember those things but only in flashes. I don't remember them thoroughly and I could forget about them. I feel there is something there, maybe a box stashed away in my mind, but I don't care to open it. It doesn't matter to me. I care about my mom, but I don't really care. We never talk. She doesn't know why I do things. My stepfather has the same way of being . . . real nice one day and fighting the next. Sometimes before I go to work, like at five in the morning, he starts yelling and swearing at me. And I just try to ignore it because that has been my weapon. Just ignore it. Close my eyes and no one can hurt me 'cause I'm not there. Seeing people shift between so many different personalities, treating you nice one day and bad the next, it messes you up and all you can think of is, What the hell did I do? Did I do something wrong? Then I look at myself and I ask, What have I done? And after a while you start thinking, I must be bad, that's what's wrong. And since I am so bad, what the hell. That's it. And you think, I don't want to be bad, but I am. Unbeknownst to me I am bad. Everywhere I look it's a mirror, I look at a bad reflection. It's hard, man! It's like, What the hell did I do, and you're always feeling guilty and stuff. And after a while you just get so much rage from all that confusion that the rage just says, OK, you are bad, so be a part of it. Like a job. Some people are born to be carpenters and maybe they don't like it, but they do it well and they might as well take pride in it.

mh: So you became good at being bad?

shank: Yeah, and I was always asking myself because, damn, this is not me! This is not me! I always fought and I tried to unleash it. I used to draw cartoons. I used to draw this character. He was on his knees looking up and he was divided down the middle. One side had a horn like a devil and the other side was like an angel. It had a halo. And on the bottom I would write, Unleash Fury. I guess it was like a subconscious call for help. Sometimes with one friend I was telling him I get so mad, and I asked him if he felt the same way. And he said, "Yeah. I feel like just going in the street and fighting and punching." He doesn't know where it comes from either, the anger. But I don't want to be bad. That's not me. I don't want to be criminal. I don't want to live fast and die young. I want to live to be a grandparent. But when I was younger, I used to think about dying. When I was nine years old. I thought life was nonsense. My father used to give me cigarettes and make me drink. I never understood it. I just felt in the way most of the time. That's the phrase I was looking for: in the way. Sometimes I would be walking down the street with my mom, and I guess I walked too slow, and she used to tug my hand and drag me and get mad. And I used to be with my father and in front of a lot of people, and someone would ask me my name and he would start jumping on me and say, "Talk like a man, talk louder—" They would laugh at me trying to smoke cigarettes. They were always partying all the time. The lights and smell of smoke . . . I wanted to do other stuff. I wanted peace and they would say no! They would force me to dance with people in the middle of the floor. I didn't even know how to dance. They wanted me to know everything. Like I was a robot. Preprogrammed . . . I used to think, Damn, I want to die. But I was too scared to pull the switch on myself.

mh: So you used to think about it?

shank: Yeah, a lot. But I never knew how. Even here. I was sick of being alone all the time. You know that feeling of being alone even though you are surrounded by a thousand people. That is like double solitude. No matter what, you will be alone. I always thought I could do it taking a lot of pills, jumping from a building. I never would have cut myself, but I used to hit myself in the head a lot. I used to ram my head into the wall and try to knock myself out. And then people made fun of that, too. I used to break things with my head. And instead of caring or doing something about it, they would all just laugh at me.

coki

it's fun being in power

I got into a lot of trouble hanging out with these

guys, but, hey, that's my team. I coulda done

that or I coulda went to school, and I'd proba-

bly be in a good college right now, but, hey, I

Coki says the only thing that's perfect in

would have missed out on a lot. I loved my

this world is a newborn baby. And he says

teenage life. I was like king of my school.

the two people he admires most in this

world arc Dr. Martin Luther King and John

Lennon because they both had impossible

dreams. He worries about the environment

and the ozone layer, and he wishes he could

work with animals, like a zoologist. *Scarface* is Coki's all-time favorite movie. He knows almost all the lines.

Coki has also been hanging out since he was about eight years old. It's not that he ever really chose to do it, but in a lot of ways, the street was a safer and more secure place for him than his house.

Coki, who was born in Ecuador but raised in Queens, has a hard time believing in himself. When he was in the seventh grade he was in the advanced students' classes, but he says he flipped on school and his grades went downhill. He ended up in special education classes for slow learners.

coki: The world was built on greed. The world runs on major power. Money power, political power, social power. It's common sense. I've known that for years. The world runs on greed and political power runs on arms, so you know the one with the most money and the most guns is the winner. That's the same way it is on the streets. The meanest guy on the block with the biggest knife or the biggest gun and the biggest pocket wins. It's fun being in power, or trying to claim the power, or trying to prove something. I used to walk into this store and walk out with cameras in my hand. When I was fourteen. I did it 'cause I knew how to get away with it. I did it because it was easy. Anything you can get away with, why not do it? You just feel smarter than the law. Especially when at home your mom is kicking and smacking the hell out of you, and all that's going on inside of you is, I hate you! Then you can't go outside with a Kool-Aid smile and be nice to everybody. I remember wanting to—I swear—to kill my mother. I remember getting smacked, punched, hit with a broomstick—boom, boom, boom—and all that's going through my head is, I want to kill you! I want to kill you!—but hey. It's not like I couldn't kick my mother's ass, physically, but you can't bring yourself up to doing it. If you did, it would be so disrespectful. No matter how much I'm getting smacked up by my mother or my father, it's not like you can just make a fist and go, boom! But you hit your kid, he'll go outside and hit someone else. How would you like to be eight years old and be thrown out of your house on a Christmas night? My parents got into a fight and my father took me with him to his

sister's house; he grabbed me and took me with him. Three days later Christmas came, and he sent me back to my mother, and she opens the door and says, "Get outta here! What do you want?" On a Christmas night! "What the hell do you want and get outta here!" I mean, I was a kid, I was a kid and I was thinking to myself, Damn! What do I do now? I'm just a kid. So I turn around and I leave and half a block later my aunt comes running after me and takes me back home. . . . There's no reason to care. You go on the street and before anybody can get close to hurt you, you gotta hurt them.

But I'm a compassionate guy. If I feel sorry for you I won't hit you. See, I think every man should have compassion, because if you don't have compassion then you're an animal. If you're an animal, then you have no control. If you have no control, you can be easily manipulated. Once you're manipulated then you're a simple soldier. A robot.

My thing was just to win. I mean, I hated everything, except winning. I hated people. But I'm a fair person and if I see that you don't deserve something bad then if I can do something about it I won't let it happen to you.

My whole life has been a whole big mess. Like trouble, fighting, screaming, yelling, every day . . . practically every day . . . I think I can honestly name only one person who cared. My teacher. And my ex-girlfriend, but I let her go.

mh: What about the crew?

coki: That was my team. That was what I cared for. That was like the family. That's who was looking out for me in the streets and that's who I was looking out for in the street. It was my other family. On the other hand my family didn't want me hanging around with all those ''criminals.'' I got into a lot of trouble hanging out with these guys, but, hey, that's my team. I coulda done that or I coulda went to school, and I'd probably be in a good college right now, but, hey, I would have missed out on a lot. I loved my teenage life. I was like the king of my school. I had the girlies and I had the respect. What mostly made me mean and mad and angry was what happened when I was like seven or eight or nine years old. Bam, bam, bam! Getting blamed for things you didn't do. Getting hit with a broomstick, bam, bam! Boom! And you being afraid of your moms and having to hide under the bed 'cause your mother was gonna get you. I was always getting blamed 'cause I was the one in the middle, between the oldest and the youngest. And I remember one day my older brother took a drill and drilled a hole in the brick wall when we lived in Ecuador. And my grandmother was after our asses. They gave my older brother a jacket so when he got hit he didn't scar or anything. But hey, I got caught for it.

mh: Were you ever scared?

coki: Can't say never. Never say never. But would I ever get scared? I don't think so. But then again, if you have no fear then there's a problem. If you have no fear it means you're not alert, you're not aware. But if you're scared, then all your senses are going. And then you catch everything. But you never let anybody know that you're scared or they think they can control you. It's good to be confident but not good to be cocky.

mh: A lot of what you're saying is how you operate in the real world, too. In a job interview you can never let them see that you're scared.

coki: That's how governments are run. Except that in the streets, it's a dictatorship, but in the United States it's a democracy. I know the whole scoop, though.

mh: What is the whole scoop?

coki: Come on! I mean, eight or nine people run like 88 percent of the country.

The crews are the same thing politically like what rules the world. The head of the crew will be the toughest guy, and then the president of the toughest crew, which is the United States, he's got the congress, and like a crew's congress is like his peers. And the gang leader might like his neighborhood to be a certain way, and the president might like his country to be a certain way. So they all use the same forms to run things in the same ways, except in

different levels of government it's much larger and it's got more power. So it's the power I look for. It's like a little boy's dream that he might go to war. When kids are born, you know, they're not born racist, you're not born dumb, you're not born bad. All these things are put into your head when you're a kid. Like boys should act like this, and boys play with soldiers and tanks and they shoot each other up. So that you grow up wanting the power because when you play with your toy soldiers, one side is going to win. And if you grow up thinking that one side won and they did it with guns, then you want that. So you think, I want to go into the military and get a gun. Maybe one day I'll go to war and win. But I guess I just didn't care enough about myself to make it happen. I realized I had a problem back when I was little and part of the problem was that I didn't care. It was like neglection. People don't realize, but the home environment does shape a kid. Like if you're in fear when you're at home that you're gonna get your ass kicked or if you're not getting your ass kicked someone in the house is getting their ass kicked or someone is fighting in the house, or else you're scared 'cause you think your parents are gonna separate or break up. It means a lot to a kid to have his parents stay together. But if you're in this constant fear you're gonna take the fear and turn it into rage and that's not good.

One day in the future, when I'm stable, I'll be happy. I know it. 'Cause no matter how much I get kicked in the face, I always get up. I can put things behind me. I have so many memories behind me now—so many bad memories, but I don't let them stop me. I don't want to be in the park when I'm like thirty years old, sipping on some juice. I ain't down with that.

there was nothing else i could do

I don't know anything about computers and

video games or music. I don't do anything. I

hang out at the handball court, but I don't do

nothing. I never even play. No sports. I'm just

IQ says he's known throughout all of New

the guy that's sitting there drinking or writing on

York City. Maybe not him, but certainly his

the walls. I think I'm boring.

tag. He was born in the Philippines and

started hanging out when he was about

twelve years old. Crews back then were

only into graffiti and dancing. The beef was

over who were the best dancers, who were

the best writers, and the fights were almost never violent. Things changed almost all of a sudden, says IQ. It wasn't enough to be a good dancer or writer, you had to know how to fight. And being a short guy, IQ was tested pretty early on. He got respect then because people could see that even though he was one of the smallest guys around, he wasn't afraid of stepping to anyone. And he usually won.

But at home, IQ was never good enough to please his parents. Unless it was an A or a first prize, everything IQ did barely got a reaction.

In 1989, IQ had one of his worst fights. Forty-first had some beef with one of its rival gangs and they had a showdown at a 7-Eleven. But that night, IQ was almost abandoned by his crew. He and two other guys were left alone to fend off an entire crew. He got hit over the head several times by someone wielding a crowbar. The doctors couldn't believe his skull hadn't been cracked open. They gave him thirty-six stitches.

On the street, Shank, Coki, and the rest of the crew said they would take one guy out from the enemy crew for every stitch in IQ's head. But IQ said enough was enough, though after losing that fight, his rep was never the same. For the first time in his life, he felt he had to carry a weapon. He doesn't believe in guns. Instead he carries a hammer in his coat pocket.

IQ got married not long after that fight and had a baby. Less than a year after his son was born, he got a divorce. Now he works in the mail room of a company, lives with his in-laws but doesn't speak to his ex-wife, and raises his son. On the weekends, IQ still chills at the park with his boys, reminiscing about the old days.

mh: How do you want to raise your son? How much do you think you'll tell him about hanging out with the crews?

iq: He's only two now. He's innocent. I don't want him to get into it. Writing on the walls, if he did that, I'd just tell him to watch out. I don't want him to get into fighting. For me, it was hard 'cause there's nothing else that I'm good at, except graffiti, and if you do graffiti, the competition starts out friendly and

then becomes violent. My brothers are into sports. A lot of the kids who play sports, that's all they're into and so hopefully he'll grow into something like that. I mean, me? There was nothing else I could do.

mh: What are you going to do for your son that's different?

iq: I'll try to be there more for him. I think my parents did a pretty good job. I mean, no one in my family has ever been arrested. For my kid, I want to do everything I can to show him I care for him 'cause I really don't think I got that from my parents. I mean, they never hit us, but if we did something bad they would just yell and not talk to us for a while. But in my kid's case I want to scold him and guide him, too. Explain to him why I'm mad. My parents never explained why they did things. I mean, I think they were good parents, but look what happened to me. I mean, they don't really know much about me. They didn't know I wrote on walls until a few years ago, and by then I was almost not doing it anymore. They didn't know who my friends were, my girlfriends, or anything. I think they're changing now with my little brothers. But they never told me about safe sex or anything, and that's why I have a kid. They should have been more supportive. Like if I was doing something good, they should praise me for it, and if I was doing bad, then I would want them to say something about it. 'Cause I used to come home drunk and stuff. Maybe they should have waited up for me. My brother sometimes had to carry me home 'cause I was so wasted.

mh: So what do you dream about for your son?

iq: I always hoped that I could afford to move to a nicer area. I mean, I live in an OK area, but these days, being a hood is in style. But maybe in a small southern town or something like that. I used to live in a small town. Maybe we should have stayed. I probably would have been completely out of trouble then. Maybe if we would have stayed there by now I'd be an artist or something. I know I did things that were wrong and I shouldn't have done things. I mean, writing on walls is OK, but there was no real reason to fight or rob people. I had money. And the fights didn't have to happen. I let them happen. I guess I did it to get a rep. And in the beginning some of my boys had never seen me fighting so they would want to see me do something. But later I didn't have to fight if I didn't want to. Then it was my choice. In the beginning, they'd see me walking and see this little man and say I was nothing. Big guys would come up to me and if I beat them down then they would remember that, and my friends would remember that. And that got me respect. Then later I would be the one that would set up the fights. People from our enemy crew would come to me and say they had a beef with one of my boys, and I would make sure to set up a one-on-one.

mh: So a lot of the times for the crew it was one-on-ones and kind of decent? No tricks?

iq: At the beginning it was bum rushes, but then both crews wanted to stop that and it was one-on-ones for a while. It's like boxing on TV. You see who's the better guy and then that's it. But if it's a bum rush then you don't know who's there and what they're carrying. Then it's not even fair. Five guys stomping on one guy. I mean, it's not good to fight, but at least one-on-ones are fair.

My little brothers have avoided it. They just have a couple of friends they hang out with, and I never hear them getting into fights or starting fights. They don't even hang out in the same spot. Like if it was me and my boys, we'd just find maybe a store or something and hang right there for maybe the whole night. Like on a corner, we'd just sit there near a phone or a store. My brothers have things to do. They do positive things. They're musicians. There's no reason to fight about music so they just don't do anything I did. We went to the same school, knew the same people, and I came out different. Maybe they were just closer to my parents than I was. Maybe they just feel like they don't have to be at the center of attention. They just do other stuff. Play video games and stuff. But I don't know anything about computers and video games or music. I don't do anything. I hang out at the handball court, but I don't do nothing. I never even play. No sports. I'm just the guy that's sitting there drinking or writing on the walls. I think I'm boring. A lot of my friends are like that, too. There's nothing that we're good at so we just hang around. And if you're good at fighting that's what you do.

I used to be good at writing graffiti, but then the city made it real difficult for us to do that. I don't like to fight anymore and I wish there was still a way to do more graffiti. It's not thrilling to

do it anymore. Now it's like secretive. I used to do it right in the daytime, right in front of people. Before, I used to do real intricate stuff and take my time 'cause I didn't care if the police would come. But now I do 'cause if I get arrested how is that gonna look to my son? Who's gonna take care of him? I don't like all of these responsibilities when all my friends are just hanging out and doing the things we used to do.

I wish I was sixteen, young and carefree. Not have to work and just get money from my parents. Back then it was easier to get away with a lot of those things. And also we were defending our territory. The reason we did that is 'cause there was really nothing else we did except hang out on that block. And as you get older you see people trying to hang out on your block and you don't like them hanging there. This block is yours, it's your property and you don't like people to step on it. If intruders leave without a fight, that's good, but if they want to fight then you have to defend it 'cause it's your place.

mh: Is it your place?

iq: No, not really. It's the city's. But that's how we feel. Say something happened, like a robbery, they'd blame us for it. But some people would stick up for us and say we were defending the block and the property. I think that's how a lot of us felt. We felt we were doing good for the block 'cause we were protecting it from outsiders. And since we were always on that block, nothing would ever happen on that block. We knew the whole block so it would be impossible for someone to get by without getting caught. But then we, 41st, got together with FTS and then it wasn't just the block, it was all of Flushing that we were protecting. And then there was competition about who was the biggest crew. Or 'cause one crew was crossing out another crew. And then it gets real big and one person's beef becomes everyone's beef.

mh: Do you think it's a good thing that kids defend their territory?

iq: I think it's a good thing that they don't like outside people damaging their area or causing trouble.

mh: Do you want your son defending . . . ?

iq: No. I just hope he doesn't even have to defend himself. I doubt he won't have to, but I hope he doesn't have to. I know he will. I guess it's just wishful thinking.

i trust the crew more than i trust any guy

I don't know why we live for when no matter

what, you're gonna die. You do get tired after

a while of having to be always protecting your-

self—watch that somebody's not gonna jump

In New York, girls have got to have a crew,

you and watch that somebody's not gonna rob

too. I hooked up with a girl crew from the

or kill you. You get tired of it.

Lower East Side of Manhattan.

I had set up my meeting for a day in

late winter and I was getting ready to leave

for it when I got a phone call from my

contact person. She told me the girls

weren't going to be able to see me. They were in a state of mourn-
ing. "Do you remember reading about a boy who was stabbed in
the heart over a pair of sunglasses?" my contact asked me. "Well,
that boy was a friend of the girls in the crew. They're very upset. I
don't think they'll be able to talk to you now. Give it a few days,"
my contact said.

The day we finally met, the girls made me wait for an hour.
Then they sauntered in. They were big girls, tall, with long hair,
huge gold earrings, red or brown lipstick, all surrounding a smaller
girl who was pushing a big, black leather baby carriage. Inside, a
tiny little boy about three months old slept soundly. At first they
walked right by me. They had expected a little old lady with gray
hair and a tattered notebook. "We never thought that people like
us, Latinos, wrote books!" they said.

That first day I met most of the girls from the crew. Cindy was
the leader. Sonya and Smooth B were seventeen-year-old twins,
both pregnant. Chris was small and soft-spoken. Nicky was the
one with the baby. The other girls took turns holding him, burping
him, feeding him (with a bottle, because they all thought breast-
feeding was kind of nasty). When the baby had to be changed,
Nicky did it where none of us could see. She didn't want us to
see his "thing." And there was Carmen: the one with the biggest
smile who hardly spoke during the several hours we ended up
meeting over the course of a couple of months. Everybody said
Carmen was the smartest, the one who got the best grades in

school, but she was also the shiest.

All of the girls were Puerto Rican and had grown up in housing projects on the Lower East Side. Their parents worked at blue-collar jobs. None of the girls spoke Spanish, but all of them except Smooth B understood it.

mh: Do you girls have a name?

smooth b: Everybody always asks us that and we say no. When we walk down the street, we pass by people, and they all say ''gangstas.'' But we don't pick a name 'cause we think it's stupid.

mh: Do most of the other girl crews have names?

sonya: Yeah, like Ridge, DOF—Destroying Our Females. We used to have names, though.

They all laugh and smile and start calling out the names they used to use: DSG (Delancey Street Girls), GIC (Girls in Control).

cindy: Like when we tag, we put LES to represent the Lower East Side.

sonya: But we had that name GIC for a long time. We used to put it up on the walls. I was Starr.

smooth b: I was always B. Now I'm Smooth B.

cindy: I was always Dee. And Carmen always used to call herself Unique.

mh: So how long have you all been a crew?

cindy: Since about third grade.

smooth b: First it was just us 'cause we all lived in the same building, and you know how when you're young you can't leave the foot of your building, and you had nowhere to go except the front of your building 'cause your mother be calling you, "Come upstairs! Come home right now!"

mh: So how many girls are there now?

smooth b: It's me, my sister, Carmen, Cindy, Chris, Marcy, Nicky, Cristina, Carmela—she's the youngest.

carmen: I'm the quietest.

sonya: Carmela is the youngest, she's twelve, but she acts mature. She wants to be like us, to be older—you know, lipstick and stuff—but we hang out with her 'cause we don't want her to hang out with other girls, 'cause her friends, they all smoke. We do, too, but we don't influence her, we don't tell her, "Here, here, smoke this," and her friends do. So she just stays with us. We used to hang out with this other girl, Aisha, but she stole money from my mother, and if she steals money from me then she's not my friend. She's just a herb. A herb is what we call nerds, weaklings.

mh: Who can be part of your crew?

cindy: People we can get along with—people we can trust. Who you can tell something to. Like if I say to Carmen I was with this guy, I know she won't go and tell someone—'cause they a lot of girls who will do that.

mh: Do you have an initiation?

sonya: No, we don't. Guys are different, they be like you have to prove yourself. With us, you don't have to prove yourself, but we'll test you. Like I'll tell her, "Oh, I slept with this guy," and if she goes and tells somebody else without asking if it's OK, then we know. So you could say we don't initiate, we just test you for your trustworthiness. There's one thing, though. If there's a new girl coming in, if anyone was to get jumped and the new girl don't jump in—then that's another thing. We're just gonna have to ban her because—well, maybe mess her up—because one of our girls got messed up, and she was there and didn't defend her.

smooth b: If someone was to mess with one of us, the next day we'll find out who's the girl and mess them up.

cindy: Yeah! We could pick on her, call her names. We could diss you so low it's not even funny. Like with Aisha. We did her so good that when she walks by us now she lowers her head down. When she used to have problems with girls she always used to come to us and say "Let's go do something," but she's a liar. She lied to her mother saying I was a big-time drug dealer, that I smoke every day, that I light her up, that I always have money. She was lying. So one day I called her a bitch and when I was walking away she called me a bitch and I yelled out, "You got crabs! Go clean yourself." But she walked away with her boyfriend.

mh: You said those things to her with her boyfriend there? Weren't you afraid he was gonna hit you back?

cindy: You crazy? No boy is gonna hit me!

smooth b: Cindy is a guy-fighter!

cindy: I don't care, you say something to me I'm gonna talk right back to you. You can be guy, girl, mother, father—if you gonna hit me, then I'm gonna have to hit you. If you try to hit me too hard then I'm gonna have to slice you. I'm not scared of nobody. If you gonna do something then you gotta do something good. You gotta beat the hell outta me like I won't remember, or kill me, 'cause, I'm sorry, if you don't kill me then I'm gonna come back and beat the hell out of you. [Pause] So, what, Maria, are you scared or something? [Laughs]

mh: No, but I'm thinking. You say you will beat up on anyone, right? How do you decide you are gonna mess someone up?

cindy: I'm not gonna hit nobody first.

smooth b: We don't start trouble!

cindy: No, but if a girl gives us a dirty look—

smooth b: She's gonna get one back—

cindy: And we gonna say something.

smooth b: Well, we do start trouble sometimes. Like, we'll walk by and see a girl we don't like and we'll be like, uugghhh. You know, we'll make her hear it so she can say something. Like when we used to get chopped, we used to just bug out and act real stupid. We act like, you know, like we don't care what happens, like the whole day is for us. One night we was all hanging out . . . Was I pregnant? Oh yeah, 'cause I remember everything that hap-

pened that night and usually when you get chopped you don't remember what happened.

carmen: We was hangin' out in the Village—

mh: You weren't making trouble that night?

smooth b: Yes we were. Those people who hang out in the Village, they've got tight jeans with holes and they got those big heels, ugly shoes—white people. You know, some of them have purple hair and they got earrings everywhere. So sometimes we walk by and make fun of them or we'll bump people on purpose and stuff like that.

cindy: And we'll be like, *"Excuse you"*—

smooth b: Most of the time when we did it we were high 'cause it's just a feeling like you in control. Nobody's in this world but you, and you have everything in the palm of your hands, so you push everybody and if they say something, you be like, yeeeaahh, what?

sonya: It's like that one day—let's say your whole week was so messed up. Friday comes and we'll all get high and bug out and it's fun—the whole weekend. Everybody says that since we got pregnant that we didn't live our life to the fullest 'cause we're so young. But they don't know how much fun we had. To me I lived it to the fullest.

smooth b: It's like the whole week you go to school, do what your mother says, do everything right, do your homework, clean, watch TV, and you know the next day you have to do it all over again. So Friday comes and there's no school on Saturday so we go and we used to hang out and act like there wasn't no law. Like we used to throw garbage cans or whatever—throw stuff at each other on the streets of the Village, throw ice when it snows, we used to chase guys. We used to beat up guys. We used to chase them and throw them on the floor—we had some good times.

cindy: Acting like we didn't care about nothing. We didn't care if we got into trouble—if anybody would say something, if we got punished—that night was our night. Every Friday night was our night. But now it's mostly me and Chris who still smoke and stuff. The others can't 'cause they're pregnant.

smooth b: You know what I like is, now that I don't smoke, when I see her get chopped I laugh 'cause I can't believe I used to do that and act that way—but if we were sober we wouldn't be doing that.

mh: But did you want to start something with people? What did you want?

cindy: Well, sometimes I would like to fight somebody. It's just a feeling . . . to show you are big enough to fight anybody.

smooth b: I learned a lot from my ex-boyfriend 'cause we used to fight like in the hallway of my old building or outside. I mean we used to *fight;* we used to be outside, and he taught me this thing that when you fight you pull the guy's shirt over their face so you hit them underneath, and I used to do it to him. He would get mad and I threw him down on the sidewalk; he used to throw me. I used to have bruises and everybody used to think he was beating me up, but it was just fun 'cause I could take it. I loved it! It was so much fun. But the girls also protect each other. Like with Cindy, we all used to think her boyfriend was no good for her. Cindy was infatuated with this guy, Shore, and she was like calling him her husband, and I knew what he was all about 'cause I used to play around with him and he used to try to kiss me and hug me, and she used to see it and get mad, but she never did anything about it. And I felt wrong. I didn't mean to do it, but I wanted her to open her eyes and see what he was doing. We're a family. We don't want to see one of our sisters get hurt.

sonya: So with the little girls in the crew we try to show them 'cause we been through it so we are like mothers to them. We don't let them smoke weed. Or they don't smoke in front of us.

cindy: Like one night with Melody, I got her real chopped and made her smoke a lot, and I want her to do that with me so I can let her realize it's not good. The reason I smoke is 'cause I got too much problems. When I smoke weed, I just don't think about things and I am just like, yeeaah, cool. . . . I get scared, sometimes, I feel like . . . but I know weed doesn't do that . . . but sometimes I feel like I'm not gonna wake up and stuff like that. Like recently, I've been thinking like the life we live is not real and all this stuff is fake. 'Cause recently everything has been happening so fast. My mother found out I was having sex, she found out I was smoking cigarettes, she found a bag of weed, and two friends passed away. So much is happening, so you keep on smoking.

smooth b: Teenagers these days have more problems than older people. Like, you know, how older people got problems, like money . . . we got money problems, too. We sixteen years old, we want things we can't have. We want everything. And we got boyfriend problems, and family. Mothers don't understand us. This is the nineties and they think it's like 1950. And mothers don't want to admit we're growing up.

mh: So, Sonya, what are the problems that you have that make you worried or upset?

sonya: Well, I don't have problems now, but I used to have problems with boys. And also 'cause I want a lot of things I can't have. These days it's more how we look than how we are inside. Before, when you were little, you wear shorts and skirts and nothing ever mattered. But now, it's like your appearance. I want clothes, jewelry, things I never had before. Like last summer when I had a pair of sneakers that were supposed to be white and they were black so I asked my boyfriend for a pair. That was when he had a job and he had some money. Last summer, before my sweet sixteen, he was selling drugs. He would sell drugs when he wanted money fast. The problem is he got greedy with it until he got arrested.

mh: What'd you feel about him selling drugs?

sonya: I didn't like it. All these guys want a fast way out instead of looking for a job—but I was scared. That was all I needed, was to lose my boyfriend in jail. But I really wanted things, you know, things I couldn't get from my mother.

smooth b: No, you just wanted things from a boy.

sonya: Because I never got anything from anybody! Like you feel special when you get little heart things. It feels good. Like he loves you, like you mean something to him. Getting something from a guy is like everything.

mh: [To Smooth B] You were also involved with a guy who was selling drugs?

smooth b: All of us have been.

mh: Well, what you told me was that part of what your crew was all about was to help each other out and keep each other going in the right direction, so how is it that you all are going out with guys who sell drugs? [They all look at me incredulously and laugh.]

smooth b: OK, look. We are teenagers, right, and we want guys our age, sixteen, seventeen, eighteen, nineteen years old. We don't go to business places to look for guys, right? We walk down the street, they rap, we take, they rap, and we find out later on that they sell. It's not like we are gonna run away and tell them no, we don't want to talk to you guys 'cause you sell, because we grew up around here and everybody we know sells. We're used to it. But it's something different if you use it. Because I know I wouldn't be with a guy who uses all those drugs, sniffing, and all that.

mh: So the guys you know who sell don't use?

smooth b: Well, yeah, but before I got together with my boyfriend, when he was twelve or thirteen, he used every drug there was and he got sent upstate 'cause of that; his mother sent him away. And so he stopped and all he does now is smoke weed. And he sells. But now I'm not with him anymore.

mh: But you're gonna have his baby.

smooth b: But we can't be together 'cause we fight all the time. The problem is that he is the type that has gotten so much stuff done to him: He was abused and everything. He is only sixteen years old and he feels like he is thirty because he has been through so much. He feels like he is so old 'cause so much things has happened to him during the years, and a lot of times he don't feel like he wants to live. His cousin died, his father died. . . . It's a lot, and then to have me on his back . . .

mh: Is he the kind of man you want to be with?

smooth b: Forever? Well, I know I can get better, but I can't blame him for doing the things he does. His mother loves him and everything, but she is on his back, too, and then me acting like I was his mother . . . He needs space now.

mh: What about you, Cindy?

cindy: Well, I didn't know that my boyfriend was doing these things. The day I met him he was all bopped up, and I didn't know what that was like 'cause all I knew about was weed, drinking, and crack. I was fifteen when I met him. And then some people told me he was doing bop and I was like, What's that? And then they told me he was selling and getting himself into problems. Even though he doesn't look like the type. He dresses nice and I thought this guy was different, but I was wrong. He used to hit me when he was bopped. Then he stopped selling and then he started again, and then I started and then we had a fight 'cause he didn't want me doing that, and he hit me and I told him to go to hell. And then he said, "OK, do what you want to do," so I kept on selling, and then I ended up owing money to the guy I was selling for. I paid him back and then I just stopped.

mh: Why did you start selling?

cindy: 'Cause I wasn't getting enough money even though I was working at an after-school program. It just isn't enough money to support me and the things I like to do. And my mother wasn't giving me enough money. But I didn't make that much money selling anyway.

mh: Have you all sold?

cindy: No, just me.

smooth b: But I used to hold material for the guys. You know, the cops know them but they got to get them, so the guys give it to us to hold and then the cops check them but they don't check us.

sonya: That was the scary part. Like when I used to hold crills in my pocket, which is crack. I used to just walk through the park, just walk away from them, but it was scary, 'cause you know if you get caught you are doing at least a couple of months in jail. I used to hold guns, too. I did it like twice.

cindy: I always hold a blade, but that's mine.

mh: But it's not like you need things really, not like you were hungry.

cindy: Why? I don't know. The extra money in my pocket and money for my weed. And I want to start again. It's the thing to have money. You know, it's fast money. It's so fast. You sell one five-dollar bag and you're making two dollars.

smooth b: But, you know, to me, when you sell weed, it's like it's not money. It's like you sell a bag because you know you can get a bag for yourself for a dollar. You sell a coupla bags and then you got money to buy some for yourself.

mh: All your friends who are supposed to be protecting you—

cindy: They have told me to stop—

smooth b: But we can't put a gun to her head and say, "Stop or I will pull the trigger." And with her, she won't get it even if you talk to her and talk to her. She won't get it through her head unless something happens to her.

mh: What will have to happen?

smooth b: Maybe go to jail or get caught with stuff on her. But if the cops find weed on you all they do is open up the bags and throw the stuff on the floor and step on it. Out here that's what they do. Or if you get caught with a lot you get a misdemeanor.

cindy: I never cared about getting caught. I don't care. I get in trouble in my house. I get screamed at and hit and I got so many problems it's not even funny. I don't want to get into that. I get in trouble and I don't care. I get in trouble for stupid things. I don't clean this or that.

smooth b: No, you're lying, and I lecture her about this. She gets herself into problems. Her mother is paying three hundred dollars a month for her to go to Catholic school, and she is messing up the last year she is going to high school. And she swears she has so many problems, well, she brings it on. Her mother fights her and I tell her to just leave it. She fights with her mother, she curses her back, her mother hits her, and she tries to hit her mother back. And I will tell her to just leave it and shut up, that her mother will get tired and stop soon, but she don't listen. And her mother punishes her and won't let her have visitors 'cause she is messing up in school, and I tell her that she only has until June and then you leave! Done with high school. She don't want to listen. She still fights with her mother. And she wonders why she gets hit, why she gets punished and picked on, why they curse at her, but I know if she was my daughter and I was paying three hundred dollars a month for her to go to school I would kill her if she messed up!

cindy: But I never asked for that! I never said to them, "Put me in this school and pay all this money—"

smooth b: Her mother and her father, they want her to make something out of herself 'cause her sister died 'cause she was in the wrong track. And when her mom found the bag of weed in her house she hit her 'cause they think she's gonna smoke weed and go to crack and then go on to the harder stuff—

cindy: It's not that I'm failing in school, I already got accepted to a local college. And I was student of the month. It's not that I'm doing badly, it's just that school got harder.

smooth b: I lecture her all the time. Like, I used to fight with my mother all the time. I used to yell at her and hit her back. I used to make my mother cry. But I stopped all that 'cause that hurts her and she don't deserve it. Your mother and father, they don't give you all you want 'cause, boom, look what you do. In school. And if they tell you to come home at a certain time—she don't come home. If I had a mother and father that were so strict, I would do what I had to do. You know, clean up my room, do good in school, so they could see that I'm a good daughter. And then I'll get what I want. She got a phone and an answering machine, this makeup thing, her own room, a TV, her own VCR, stereo, a bedroom set.

cindy: I got everything.

mh: But you still want to sell some weed?

cindy: I've always got to have money. Even if it's just two dollars in my pocket. And I like to have things done my way. Like if I want to go out, you gonna have to let me go or else I'm gonna have a fight. You see, I'm the bad one: Cindy doesn't do this or that. They try to keep me in the house all the time. I have to do all the cleaning. Sometimes I say I'm gonna run away, but I can't 'cause I got no place to go. We argue a lot at the house. Not long ago they were arguing because some film from a camera got lost, and they were all yelling at me 'cause they thought I had lost it, like it was a big deal. And I said it seemed like the film was more important than me. And then they were saying that one of my friends took it. And meanwhile my sister had it, and I was crying and then my father started screaming at me for no reason. And then on Friday my father hit me 'cause I didn't clean my room. When they hit me I hit them back. Not like I want to, but to protect myself. You scream at me, I'm gonna scream right back, and they all know that. Violence is a way to live. That's the way you gotta live. You know, like even if a guy comes and he's twice your size and he says "Shut up" you have to say "No, you shut up."

smooth b: Like if my boyfriend says, "I don't want you to be here while I'm selling," I would leave. But if he tells me to stay home all day or don't come outside, I'll be like OK, but then I'm right out the door after he leaves 'cause no way I'm gonna stay at home 'cause he says so. My mother doesn't tell me to stay at home so why should some guy? The guys think that once they got a girl they can say, like, "Stay home, stay home." Sometimes it's not to hurt them but to keep them. Like girls do the same thing. They say don't go there or do this 'cause they don't want to lose them.

cindy: My ex-boyfriend used to do that. He would tell me what to do, to stay home and stuff—

smooth b: And she used to do it. And I used to tell her, "Yo, he is taking over your life," but she wouldn't listen.

cindy: Well, even so, he used to call me a lot. Sometimes he would call me at three in the morning. Anytime he called I was there.

smooth b: You know what's funny? We're tough to everybody, to the world, with people we hang out with. But when it comes to a boyfriend-girlfriend relationship, we're weak. We're not as strong as everybody thinks we are.

sonya: We are so eager to find somebody to tie down with—

smooth b: To have somebody love us besides our mother and father and friends, to be sexual with somebody. To feel warmth and be loved by somebody. With our guys, we are weak. But with the guys we hang out with and the girls out there, we are tough.

————

"I trust the crew more than I trust any guy," says Cindy. Even though they all spend a lot of time talking and thinking about boys, Cindy and Carmen said they know that the boys only talk to them when the boys want something from them.

One day I met with only Carmen and Cindy. It was the first day Cindy let down her guard, opened up, and showed her vulnerability. That was the day Cindy told me that the day she was born her father cried because he had wanted a boy. That was the day Cindy told me that she often thought about dying, that she wanted to leave New York City but was scared of the loneliness she would have to face without her friends.

cindy: I am tired of this life. Sometimes I'll be like, I want to kill myself. 'Cause I don't know why we live for when no matter what, you're gonna die. I mean, you can be the worst person in the world and you can still be alive, and you can be the best person and you die. That's not right. Why you gotta be all perfect if you're gonna die anyway? You get tired after a while of having to be protecting yourself—watch that somebody's not gonna jump you, watch that somebody's not gonna rob you or kill you. You get tired of it. But at the same time, if I'm gonna get hurt I want to get hurt. If it's a fair fight I don't want anybody else to jump in. 'Cause if they jump in then my crew jumps in. If I fight you then it's you and me. If not it gets bigger and bigger. And I hate that.

mh: What about you, Carmen?

carmen: Well, if somebody says something to me I'm gonna say something back. But if somebody steps on me and they say sorry I'll be OK and that's it.

mh: So what makes Cindy the way she is? I mean, Cindy is one of the leaders of the crew and she carries the attitude with her. Why does the crew have to be like that? What else could the crew be like?

carmen: It could be all of us hangin' out and being friends instead of being so mean. But that's the way it's got to be down here. Even at home. Like, my father, he'd be cursing and stuff. He tells me to shut the hell up and calls me a little bitch and a *cabrona*.

cindy: But they don't mean it. It's just that at the spur of the moment when they're mad they say that. Like my father. He does that. He'll say, "*¡Tú eres tan puta! Tú no haces esto, cabrona. ¡Hija de la gran puta!*" But he doesn't mean it because if he meaned it I would have been out a long time ago. With so much stuff I do to them and I am still in the house. I know girls who hit their parents. Like I hit my mother once and it was a reaction, like someone is gonna hit me and I'm gonna hit them back. It wasn't intentional. It's just that she went to punch me and so when she hit me I just reacted and I pushed her. Then she went to her room and told the girls to leave. Then she told me I couldn't go outside but then later she let me go. You know they say that parents abuse and hit their kids? But the way my mother and father hit me I don't call it abuse. I don't because they have a reason to hit me and I know it.

mh: What do you think is a good reason to hit you?

cindy: 'Cause I'm stupid. They're trying to teach me right from wrong. I mean, my father hits me 'cause of my room, that's because I'm stupid. We're always arguing. But he's sweet, too, he gives me money. Now, I'm waiting for his income tax to come in 'cause I'm gonna go crazy with that money. I'm gonna buy me a leather jacket and a pair of jeans. I have to have nice new sneakers, new boots, new jeans, a nice shirt—

mh: Well, some people just don't have money and that's the way it is. What about just accepting it?

cindy: I can't. I just can't have the same shirt every day and the same jeans. To be who I am I have to have everything nice. A girl who is nice. A girl who has everything. And I do have everything. I have a phone. The twins don't have a phone in their house. I have a phone in my house and a phone in my room. Now I don't have the phone 'cause I'm grounded, but I know I'll get it back. 'Cause that's the way they are. They say I'm grounded and can't have visitors but all my friends come over. Like right now I'm grounded 'cause of school and I'm failing. Ever since I was little they let me do whatever I wanted to do. So I took advantage. I feel like all my father's money is my money. Even though I don't work for it.

mh: Would you want another family?

cindy: No. But my sister passed away and that was my favorite sister. I was thirteen at the time. She used every drug there was.

She was no saint but she had a good heart. But if you stepped on her you were messing with the wrong person. She's like me. She used to beat up people for nothing. She used to steal from stores. She was the best thief! She used to steal from good stores, nice clothes, nice shoes. Don't ask me how. People who use drugs, they can do things. But if you look at her she didn't look like the kind of person who used drugs. Before she got bad, she used to be beautiful. Straight hair, blond hair. She used to go everywhere from here to Mexico 'cause her friends were big-time drug dealers. That was the kind of person she was. Sometimes I hate God, even though I'm Catholic and stuff, I hate him because he takes away so many good people. Like Raul, Gordo, and Yvonne, my sister. They don't deserve it. Meanwhile there are worse people who are killing people and they are still alive and these others who never did nothing to nobody—they die. My other sister is the angel in the house. She gets awards for being so smart. And that's what I hate. They are always comparing me to her and I don't appreciate that. I'm not her. I'm Cindy and they don't understand that.

Maybe I bring it on myself. I have time to study but I'm too lazy. I don't feel like I have time to study; I have better things to do. But then you realize, like, damn, this is your life . . . you got to work and you got a future. Not to sound all stupid and stuff but I wish I was dead. It's true. I told Smooth B and she gets mad 'cause I write her letters where I say I wish I could kill myself. 'Cause this life, it's stupid. You gotta be a fighter and stuff. Now

I'm scared I'm gonna start crying. I mean, I don't like it. I don't like being in my house, I don't like school. . . . These are things I keep to myself, but I told Smooth B 'cause I was tired of keeping it in so long. Like all these people were dying, and at nighttime I cry and I hear songs and think of Gordo and everybody. Too many innocent people are getting hurt. My mother wants to send me away. Like my sister is moving to Missouri and I want to move but then I don't. I want to stay here, but then I don't, 'cause so many people are gonna be dying soon and everybody knows it, and I don't want to be around to see that. One of my close friends died and my sister and it's not right. It's hard. It's really hard. God forbid, if my crew died, I would die with them. Like if Smooth B

died I would kill myself. She's my best friend even though I never tell her how much I care for her. She's the only sister I have. And Peter, the guy I call my brother—if something happens to him, I'll go crazy. Things happen to the wrong people, and I just want to get away from here, but then I don't. I don't. I don't want to leave the girls. I want to represent the Lower East Side. I'm here and I want people to know how it is to be out here. Now I guess I'm able to deal with it. I won't kill myself, I guess. Sometimes when I would have a big argument in the house, I would look in the mirror and say, Damn, I want to kill myself. But I don't know if I have the heart to do it. I've been taught in Catholic school that it's a sin and no matter what you go straight to hell, and I wouldn't want to go to hell. Not forever. Not ever.

I met the girls once right after they had gotten out of school. They were unrecognizable. They were wearing pink button-down shirts, plaid skirts, white tights, and polished black shoes. Cindy and Carmen go to Catholic school. Carmen teaches religion classes on Sunday. Cindy failed her religion class in school, and so on Sundays she spends several hours studying Catholicism.

The girls observe Lent. They pray. They bless each other. When they walk by a church they genuflect and cross themselves.

One day, after our meeting, I was saying good-bye and getting ready to walk several blocks to the subway. They all gave me kisses on the cheek and said good-bye. But before I turned away to make my trek, all of the girls came up to me and surrounded me. They made sure my lipstick was on straight. They told me not to forget my umbrella. They fixed my hair and said, "Be careful when you get on the subway. It's dangerous. If anything happens, just call us. We'll be there for you." And then they said, "*Vaya con Dios.*" Go with God.

mh: What is the difference between a boy crew and your crew?

smooth b: We're more of a family. Like sometimes when we get mad we talk about each other behind our backs, but it all gets out in the open later on. But with them, if one finds out the other is doing something they all try to kill each other, and they supposed to be friends. Like the guys around our neighborhood, one guy is killed and later on you find out who did it—

chris: Their best friend. Girls can handle their situation better. They know how to calm themselves down and guys, right away, they got more of a temper. But when it comes to our boyfriends—

cindy: It's like, "You can't do this, you can't do that, you got to stay home, who do you think you are? Gangsters? You think you're gangsters? No, no, no. Go home, go home." That's what our boyfriends say to us.

chris: Our boyfriends think we are so sweet, stay home and hang out with our friends . . . but they don't realize what we do.

smooth b: They don't know half of what we do. And our boyfriends, they don't realize that we have guy friends. They don't like that. Especially if they are from another neighborhood. Like if you're going out with someone from Avenue D and you hang out with some guys from the hill, they don't like that. They think right away that we have something going with one of them.

chris: But in our crew it's not only girls. Before it was like girls keep their own crew and guys keep their own crew. Now it's like guys and girls. If anything happens to us we get a guy crew to kick a girl's ass or jump her. Even guys will come to us and say, "Yo, I want you to go and kick this girl's ass," and we will go and kick her ass. The crews are now more combined. We look out for each other.

smooth b: But one time, when my ex was getting into a fight with this boy, I got in so I could stop him, 'cause I didn't want him to hit the kid, and he went and punched me instead of the kid. He got me right here in my jaw.

mh: The way you talk it's like there are fights every single day.

cindy: Not every day, but every week. We're cutting school tomorrow. We're gonna go fight this girl Smooth B's ex is going out with. Me and Carmen are going to go pick up Chris to fight with the girl. We're gonna scare her first. Then I'm gonna get down and punch her. I don't want Smooth B's ex with anybody else, even though he wasn't my boyfriend.

chris: The thing is that these girls all know Smooth B is having a baby with him, and they all are going out with him.

cindy: We're gonna go outside and say, "We see you talking to Danny," and if she says yeah, then we're gonna say, "Well, look, this is Danny's ex-girlfriend. She's having a baby. Do you know that?" We're gonna scare her.

mh: Are you gonna take something with you?

all: We always do!

mh: What?

cindy: My blade.

mh: And are you, Chris, gonna get a knife?

chris: From a friend's house. But we'll just use it to scare her.

cindy: I hear she's only thirteen years old but she thinks she's bad.

chris: We could all get in trouble. But I don't care. Let's say she is thirteen and we are all sixteen, seventeen, eighteen. She could press charges and we could get in trouble for trespassing in her school. But she won't know who we are.

mh: But the thought of getting in trouble, the thought of her pulling something out and slashing you, the thought of her hitting you in your belly—

smooth b: I just don't think it will happen.

chris: You can't tell how a person is. Maybe she looks all nervous after we start talking to her and then we'll just let her go. But if she's gonna talk back, with her attitude, then that's when you know. She's got the balls to do that, then you might as well hit her.

mh: Is this the only way to resolve things on the street? Scare them, pick a fight, pull out your blade?

smooth b: It's not really to pick a fight. You just tell them to stay away from whoever you want. I get scared to fight, 'cause I can get out of control and I might kill somebody. That's why I don't like to fight. 'Cause I got a lot of anger inside of me. A lot happened to me in my life so I'll take it out on someone.

chris: Like me and my sister, she thinks she can rule, and one day we got into a really big fight and I had so much anger in me I thought I was gonna kill her. I took her and picked her up and threw her against the table.

smooth b: Like me and Sonya. We used to fight—slapping and kicking.

mh: What's all the anger?

smooth b: [Quiet at first] I don't know. Everything, my whole life.

chris: I know I got so much anger. They say you should talk to somebody or whatever to deal with your anger. But I know if I carry a gun, a knife, a blade, and someone was to step to me, I know I'd kill them.

cindy: I'm gonna buy a gun for $150.

smooth b: I wanted to get one, too.

chris: It's the anger, I know. But my intention is not to kill somebody 'cause I don't think I'm gonna waste my life in prison for somebody.

cindy: It's not for using it. It's to have it.

smooth b: I wanted a gun but now I don't.

mh: Why did you want one in the first place?

smooth b: It's fun. Like you ever watch rap videos and the song "I Want a Gangsta Bitch." You see how she goes and she's shooting in the park with her boyfriend. I like that a lot. And she goes up to a girl and takes her earrings 'cause she got a gun. I like that. That's why I wanted it. But see, in the video, it's free, they could do it 'cause it's a video, but outside, it's different. You shoot up in the air, the cops catch you, and that's it.

chris: I don't want one 'cause my temper is so bad I'll end up hurting somebody.

cindy: I want one. I'm gonna get it in two weeks. It's small. I'm gonna buy it from a friend of mine. I was at his house and we saw the video and I was like, "Yo, yo, I want one." And I thought he was playing around. He was telling me all the types he could get. He had a tech nine, a twelve-shooter. He didn't show it to me, but I know he has it 'cause they be shooting around the block. A lot of guys from around the block got them. In my building they have them and so he said, "What kind do you want?" And I was like, "I want a small one." And he said he got a six-shooter and I was like, yeah. It comes with six bullets. But that's nothing 'cause I won't even use the bullets. I'll leave them home. I'll take one bullet. Inside. 'Cause if somebody says something to me I'll pull it out and say, "What?" and then they'll get scared.

chris: Not the guys down our way! They'll be like, "You want to shoot?" And they'll kill you before you pull it out.

mh: So what do you think about Cindy buying a gun?

smooth b: I ain't gonna be with her if she gets a gun—

cindy: You're gonna be the first one to tell me to let you hold it! You were the first one who wanted one—

smooth b: Exactly, you got it! *Wanted* one. I don't want one no more. I don't like them now. For what? What she gonna carry one for? You ain't gonna use it? I doubt it. I'm having a kid. You think I'm gonna walk around with my kid and she got a gun on her? What if it falls on the ground or something and they catch you right there, and if I'm with you, they're gonna take my kid away from me. You crazy? To risk all that . . .

mh: But not too long ago you wanted one.

smooth b: Having a kid changes all that. It's real stupid to have one.

chris: I don't see myself getting a gun 'cause all I see are my friends dying. And then I'm gonna be just another person killing my own friend maybe just 'cause I'm gonna be carrying a gun. I can't do that. I'm upset 'cause everyone is carrying them and dying over stupid stuff. The most we can do is give Cindy advice. She don't take it—we're doing our job as friends trying to give her advice. If she don't take it, she on her own.

mh: But the whole thing about a crew is that you aren't on your own. You back each other up.

chris: I guess a lot of people don't back up anybody these days. We do. We will stick with you to the end if we see you are doing something *right,* but if we feel you are doing something wrong and you're gonna try to take us down with you, no. A crew is to stay up. Not to go down with you.

cindy: You crazy? I'm not gonna use it!

smooth b: So why would you pay $150 to get it? If I'm gonna pay $150, I'm not gonna put it on my shelf for display.

mh: When I was asking you about the anger that you have, what do you think about that brings it out?

chris: I get angry with death. My anger comes out with death. Every time somebody dies I'm like with the question, Why? And I think about my mother leaving me, 'cause she is sick, too. I get scared. Real scared.

smooth b: I feel a lot of anger towards God. I swear I do. I believe in him, I pray to him every night, but I don't like him.

cindy: It's wrong of him to do what he does.

chris: It's not the sense of him being wrong. He put us on this earth and he just left us on our own. It's not his fault just because he rules us.

smooth b: But that's how you look at it. He could tell the future. He does the future. Why would he put a little boy or girl on this earth to die so young? Like you see little babies buried in the cemetery. If he is so much God like everybody says and he could forgive and all of that, why does he put kids on this world so that at the age of fifteen, twelve, ten, just to die? He could make it so that if you're about to kill someone then he can make the gun fall, or make you run away. He could have stopped it!

chris: But I'm still living and I'm not gonna blame him.

cindy: But why is he putting us through the pain we got now?

chris: So are we gonna blame God for Raul, who died two weeks ago? God gave him a chance and he ended up killing himself.

smooth b: All right, I don't know about people killing themselves, but to kill somebody else for some stupid reason—

chris: But we made ourselves like that—

smooth b: Yeah, it's our fault, too.

mh: But at the same time, you all talk about being excited 'cause you are gonna go beat up someone, you're talking about carrying a blade, talking about getting a gun—

chris: To me, all my friends are dying and I am stressed out. There can be times that all I want to do is cry all day 'cause of everything that is going on. Since the funeral, I slept with my mother for a whole week. I was scared.

smooth b: I didn't cry that much for him. I just keep thinking like he's alive.

cindy: The thing with Gordo started a long time ago, like when he was in fifth grade. Gordo always bullied the guy who killed him. Now they came after him after Gordo had knocked out this one guy's tooth, and he told him it wasn't going to end there. So one day, Gordo came to school with a pair of Mickey Mouse glasses so the boy took the glasses. So Gordo went up to him after class and said, "Give me my glasses," and the guy said, "You dead on the glasses, you dead on the glasses," so Gordo started punching him in the face and the guy pulled out the knife from his back pocket and he stabbed Gordo in the leg, and when Gordo went to punch him again, he stabbed him in his heart. They say he fell face first and he was bleeding. They say the ambulance didn't come for a while. It happened in the junior high school, in the hallway. The board of education paid for the whole funeral. The day it happened, when Smooth B first came up to get me and she was crying, I thought maybe she had lost the baby or something, God forbid. But when she told me I kept telling her to stop playing, that it was no joke. And then I realized it was true, and then we went back to his building and stayed in the hallway two days. We would go home late at night and then come back early in the morning and stand in the hallway the whole day. That was where all his friends were.

smooth b: We all made this big wooden thing with his tag on it. His tag was "Best." We all signed it. And all the movie cameras were there and stuff.

mh: Was it the first time that somebody close to you was killed?

They all say no. They all have other friends from the neighborhood who have been killed. They mention Raul, the young boy who is said to have committed suicide four days after Gordo's death.

smooth b: They say he was hangin' out with a coupla friends and he was bopped up, and I guess he had been having problems with his family and friends, and one guy walked him home and he said, ''I love you and my mother,'' and he shot himself in front of his friend.

mh: So you have been through two deaths in less than a week.

smooth b: And a coupla months before this, Pizza, our other friend, was killed by the police. He was shot at the video store.

cindy: And two years ago my sister died, but it wasn't violent. The violent deaths are the worst. 'Cause just before Gordo passed I was talking to him on the phone.

chris: Usually I'm not afraid of death, but I was so stressed even my mother noticed it. I was even scared to walk my dog.

smooth b: Now since Gordo died they say my ex-boyfriend is next, they say his best friend is next, his brother is next and another guy we know. They were all involved with the fight, too, so that's why they are saying that. But Gordo's is the last funeral I am going through. I didn't even want to go to Raul's.

cindy: When I went to Raul's funeral I didn't cry much. I guess because of so much that I had cried for Gordo. I still cry every day.

I hear the songs he used to like and I start crying.

chris: I don't think I have the tears no more. All of my tears are wasted. Now I cry in the inside. For me, there is like a question mark on my heart. Who is next?

smooth b: It's bad to be so young and be going through all this. I mean, we are supposed to be having fun. Not to have a lot of people die.

cindy: Even the week before Gordo died we were going out, we had fun.

smooth b: Now I feel like if I go out and have fun, it's disrespectful to Gordo.

mh: Would Gordo's death make you think twice about doing something violent to someone else because you saw what happened to him?

smooth b: No.

cindy: It wouldn't stop me.

chris: Me either.

mh: I'm not saying you would want to take somebody's life, but you talk that way—what about that? Then the guy's life or girl's life that you take, their crew, their friends, would be sitting around a table like we are, saying things like you—that they cried for five days, and how sad they are, and asking themselves Why, why, why?

smooth b: It's true, it's true. I know what you're trying to say. You're saying that the guy who killed Gordo, Johnny, probably killed him out of all of the anger that he had 'cause Gordo was always picking on him . . . like when we pick on people. But we don't see it like that since it was our friend that died. We don't see the fact that Johnny was probably fed up and mad 'cause since the fifth grade Gordo had been picking on him. He probably didn't even mean to kill him, but it just happened. But we don't see it like that. If it was him who got killed and not Gordo, then it would be the other way around. His friends would think that Gordo did it 'cause he wanted to, and Gordo probably would have done it only 'cause he was mad at the kid. Do you get it?

mh: I get it, but what I don't understand is this: You all say that you are depressed and stressed out and wondering about when the next call about another one of your friends is going to come. . . . At what point do you say, "I'm not going to be violent. I'm not gonna go up to this girl and slap her because that is the way it started with Gordo."

chris: Instead of preventing that stuff we are doing the same thing. But we don't see it that way. It's like we have blinders on. It's like we are just as bad as he is.

smooth b: It's true, we are just as bad. But we just don't see it like that.

cindy: I don't doubt that somebody else is gonna die. Especially this summer. If it doesn't happen it will be an incredible miracle.

chris: You know what it is? There are a lot of older guys in jail, and they are gonna come out and try to rule all over again, and everything is gonna happen all over again. This crowd is gonna try

to take over this crowd, and then when that crowd comes out of jail they will combine with these guys and start all over again, and then we are just gonna have to dress in black again.

smooth b: Well, I ain't dressing in black no more. Sorry.

mh: Well, what are you gonna do about it?

cindy: We can't do nothing about it.

chris: It's not like we killed somebody.

cindy: It's not like we could go back in time and rewind it and then make sure we do things right. We can't do nothing now. We're not gonna be all out in the street saying, change your mind over this and change your mind over that. We're just gonna go on with ourselves—

chris: And just keep looking out for each other.

cindy: That's it. That's all we can do. I'm not gonna change just 'cause one person died. He was special to us. But I don't think even he would have wanted us to change.

everything i got, i paid for

Just one day they came and took us away. Just

like that. Word. Some white lady came. And

we ended up all the way in Long Island. I didn't

know what was going on, but I was excited at

When we first met, Tre, who had just

first. Until a coupla days went by and we never

turned eighteen, was wearing his old con-

went home.

struction work clothes and a gray hoodie

pulled up and shadowing his eyes. Every-

thing about Tre seemed gray that day. His

clothes were gray, his face looked gray, he

mumbled when he talked. But he told me

a few stories and made me laugh. We hit it off well. We talked about his crew. He said it was the only thing he had in his life. They didn't have a name, but they were down 'cause they all hung out on the same street in the Bronx. Tre and many of his boys had known each other since they were toddlers. Then Tre left the neighborhood for almost ten years. When he came back, although other things had changed in the 'hood, his boys were still there. But his crew had been reduced to just five guys. The rest were in jail, in wheelchairs, or dead.

That rainy morning, Tre told me how it always surprised him how easy it was to make money "in ways that no one gets hurt." He liked doing that stuff better than getting paid by jumping people, which at one point, he and his crew did. "I'm talking about white-collar crime," he said. He explained that white-collar crime is when he would get dressed up, "like the way people do downtown when they go to work." Then he would go into a restaurant with a friend, sit down, and order some food. He would spot someone's handbag, take it, and walk out nonchalantly. Other times he would go to the bars downtown and put his coat over another guy's and walk out with both. He couldn't believe that people were "stupid enough" to carry that much money in a coat or bag and leave it unattended. Once he found four hundred dollars in a trench coat. I asked him if he felt bad about taking other people's money. "Nobody gets hurt when I do that stuff. And besides if they carry so much money like it don't mean nothing, then they deserve it. I need the money more than they do, right?"

He learned the tricks of white-collar crime from his father.

tre: I was seven when I was taken away from my parents. There was ten of us. We all got divided up. We got moved to Hempstead, Long Island. We were put into foster care. I was with my two brothers. We were just wild on the street. We were in school and everything, but we were just being bad. Then I got a little older and I got put into a group home. I ran away from there and I started selling drugs in Long Island. Made a little money. Then I wanted to get large so I came back up to Manhattan, and that's when I got back with my old crew.

mh: How much do you remember about what happened that day when you were seven years old?

tre: I remember the day they was taking us away, this lady came and took us in the car. I didn't know what was going on. Just one day they came and took us away. Just like that. Word. Some white lady came. And we ended up all the way in Long Island. I never even heard of Long Island. We just out there and the foster parents—they used to beat on us. The money they used to give them for us, they ain't never used it for us, so we never had no clothes or nothing. So it was just me and my brothers. One older and one younger. I didn't know what was going on but I was excited at first. Until a coupla days went by and we never went home. And I didn't hear from my moms after that till I was fifteen.

mh: So what happened in those foster homes?

tre: The first one we was in, the man used to beat us, me and my little brother. I just couldn't stand it. They wasn't my real parents. So I was just wilding and they used to send me from foster home to foster home, and finally they broke me and my brother up. I just kept going from foster home to foster home and after a while, not too many foster homes wanted me anymore. So they put me in this detention center way out deep in Long Island. Real deep in Long Island. It was called St. Mary's. I was there for about three months. They told me they was putting me in a group home for acting up. I was supposed to be there for six months but I was only there for three months, then I went AWOL. I was thirteen and I was living in the street with my man for about a year, selling drugs. They never even came to look for me. And I was on the same block I was on when they picked me up. All the time in the same place. And DSS [Department of Social Services], I thought they were gonna come and look for me but they never came either. . . . Yeah, now my whole family is split up because of the foster care system. I don't know where two of my sisters is at. My little brother is in Long Island. He adopted by my aunt. I don't see him much. My aunt, she buggin'. She wanted to adopt me, too. But back then I was having fun, making a little money. I was only thirteen, and I was making money. I was just going with the flow. I was still going to school, still enrolled. I was going to high school. I passed ninth grade and did a week of tenth. After that week of tenth, I just left and didn't ever come back. Started drinking beer and smoking cigarettes and smoking weed on the same day. And we used to just sit in the yard all day. Crackheads come in the yard and buy it and then leave. I remember I felt like I didn't have nowhere to go. I was following everybody else. I didn't know what to do. I was scared. So I was just doing what my brother was doing. I was expecting to be in jail though, by now. I was just lucky. But as soon as we left Long Island, my brother got arrested. I was scared of the whole business of drugs. I didn't know nothing about selling drugs. I was getting drunk, all like that. I was too young for that. At least I wasn't smoking crack. And then I felt hurt. I didn't know where my moms and my pops was. Then when I found out where they was I didn't come right on up here 'cause I felt like they didn't want me to, 'cause they ain't never tried to keep in contact with me. I still don't know my moms and my pops. I mean, I know who they are, but I can't sit down and talk to them. I live with them, but I do my own thing. But if I didn't have this construction job-training program I would be doing nothing. Just chilling all day. After this program ends I'll be doing the same thing I was doing before. Hustling. Just trying to keep clothes on my back. Word. The only reason I ain't sad now is 'cause I am doing this construction. I got something to do.

mh: So let's take it back. You are in this crack house— What do you remember?

tre: Well, one time, you know how you selling drugs, I ran out of my packages. All the money I was making, like every time I made a sale, I took the five dollars and bought me some beer or some weed, so my money was gone. So I started selling dummies. You know how you buy peppermint in the store? I was sucking the red stuff off and chopping it up and putting flour on it and making it look like crack. One time I was selling to this lady and she almost bought the dummies and her friend, this girl, came up to me and was swinging this butcher knife at me. I didn't know what to do. I couldn't run nowhere. It was a woman, though. So I just went upside her head. I didn't want to do that. I felt bad about it after that. But she came at me with that knife and she scared the death out of me. That was the scariest thing that ever happened to me out there.

mh: And there was no one out there to help you?

tre: There was my homeboys there, laughing. Bugging out. My brother wasn't there. He was in jail.

mh: She was trying to kill you and they were laughing?

tre: Yeah, they was laughing. See, I was about to sell the dummies, but the cops rolled by so I gave the dummies to this girl to hold, and she ran off thinking she had gotten some real crack, and then when her friend found out they were dummies her other girlfriend came back at me and started yelling at me about the dummies. I told her to get outta there and then she just spit in my face. I had these sunglasses on and she spit right on them, and then she pulled out the knife. My homeboys was laughing and I was all drunk and scared. What if I would have slipped or something? That would have been it and they was all laughing. Word . . . Police was chasing me for a week for doing that to that lady. She went and pressed charges and stuff. Her face looked all messed up. Thinking about that now, I was lucky. 'Cause you know how you be doing stuff and you be thinking how it's gonna come back at you . . . that's gonna come back to me . . . I shouldn't have did that. I should have just ran. If she didn't spit in my face I may have just run or just smacked the knife outta her hands. But she spit in my face! I wasn't thinking about nothing after that. That was it. Word. I felt real bad. But I didn't let nobody know I felt bad. I was popping a lot of stuff like how she shouldn't have done that and blah de blah. But I was feeling bad inside. That's probably why I am the way I am now, all messed up. Word.

After this construction program I ain't got nothing to do. No job. No nothing. People say they gonna help you get a job, but the truth is, ain't nobody ever do nothing for me. Ever since I was seven years old ain't nobody ever give me nothing. Since I was seven years old, nobody ever bought me a pair of sneakers or socks, nothing. Everything I got, I paid for. Everything. I was paying rent when I was thirteen. Fifty dollars. May seem like nothing, but I was paying rent. Who else at thirteen paying rent? Making money like that. We was bugging. Funny thing about it. The reason why I left Long Island 'cause after I make all that money, I was smoking too much weed and drinking. I was drinking Cisco and beer and

Bacardi and I wasn't buying no more clothes. I was just buying beer and weed and that's all I was doing. So I came back uptown. I bet if they wouldn't have taken us away I probably would have finished school or something. I wouldn't been doing what I am doing now. It would be a whole different thing. Humph. I mighta been a sucker. Shoot, I'd rather be a sucker than how I am now 'cause I ain't got nothing now. Eighteen years old and I ain't got nothing. You know. Word . . . You be seeing people eighteen years old, my age, and they got jobs, a car, chilling. I ain't got nothing. Little bit of money I make in this construction, I could go home and make it in one night.

But I ain't doing it like that no more. I don't want to go to jail. I ain't never go to jail yet. It would be stupid for me to go to jail now 'cause it would be too late by the time I come out. So I don't want to go to jail. But when I got back from Long Island I got back with my old crew. I hooked up with my man.

You know how in the crews, out of the whole crew, you may be cool with just one person, real cool with just one person, out of all of them. Me and my man, we tight. I don't know why, we just tight. We used to go out and just be robbing and stuff— without the crew. I don't know what we was thinking about. And we don't even need the money. Just doing it just to be doing it, just so we could say that we did it. Yeah, like we would say, "You see that punk, we did him."

I don't know what to do, every time he asks me, I can't say

no. What I gonna look like saying no? He never say no to me. Then if I say no, he still gonna go do it by himself anyway, and then it's gonna be like I ain't looking out for him and that I don't care if he gets caught or nothing. I could tell them no if it's something stupid where I know we might get caught or get hurt or something. Anytime I asked them, like if I needed help, like if I might ask them to do something they didn't think was too tough, they still went along with it anyways, so I guess I gotta do the same thing. What happens is that your crew disowns you. Basically. Not like disown you, not really. But then they look at you like, "He a little punk. He lost his heart." They might say something like that or they might not say anything, but that's what's circulating. You might not hear it, but that's what's being said. They say, "He soft, he a little punk, he ain't got no heart." Then they be saying, "Damn, that's his own crew dissing him." They might try to come and rob me or something—do some fake moves like that. Then my crew be walking around saying, "Tre is fronting on us." Or they might be at a party and start saying I fronted on them and calling me a sucker and all that, and somebody may just be there that I have a beef with, and then they know I ain't down with the crew no more, and they think that's the perfect time for them to come with they little posse and do their little thing. But that's not really what I'm worried about because if that happens then, damn, I can handle myself by myself. Still, I just gotta be cool 'cause what am I gonna do without my crew? Unless I got a job or something and I'm about to move off the block, what I'm gonna do? Am I about to move off the block? Not right now. And I can't just tell them no 'cause when this program is over then I dissed them, so now I'm supposed to come back all two-faced and say wassup? Now that I ain't got no job no more, now I want to be down with them again? It don't work like that. I be feeling like, yo, man, we should stay as a crew, man, but we just need to get some jobs, man. Word. It's time for people to go legit. All my homeboys either got murdered or in jail. Come on now. And they still want to do all the same old things like back in the days. It ain't like back in the days no more. All of us getting older. Like my man, he doing a little construction work. But that be the one I be doing robberies with. He trying to get hisself together, but he still in this little robbery thing for some reason. He always be like that, ever since he was fourteen and he first moved on the block he been a little stick-up kid. Fourteen years old and sticking people up. See he's younger than me but he's big and real tall. So he be running up on people and he be putting them to sleep, throwing them in the yoke, and putting them right to sleep and taking their money. Just like that.

mh: Putting them to sleep?

tre: You never heard of the sleeper hold? You grab somebody by the neck and push they neck up and out and they fall asleep. I don't know how we learned that . . . watching it on TV . . . and then we just do it. When you rob people you just put that little pressure and hold it for a while and then you feel them go down.

But I be thinking about stuff now—'cause I'm ready to get my life together, to tell you the truth. I'm tired of all that. I know I'm lucky I ain't never been to jail, and I probably committed every crime possible. I been arrested but never been to jail. You know why I never been to jail? 'Cause every single time, let's say the police run up on the crew, every single time, they might arrest everybody in the crew but me, but what they do to me, they take me somewhere, beat me down, and let me go. Every single time— it never fails. I don't have to say nothing! I just keep my mouth shut and they look at me and say, "Oh, you a wise guy! Oh, you a hard rock!" And I'm just looking like nothing—and they give me the beat-down and then they let me go. Every time. But then again, this lady cop once let me go. I got caught with a gun and everything and she let me go. Just from me talking to her. She chased me and I threw the gun, and she caught me and the gun. I told her I didn't know what to do. I told her everything, my whole life story. She took the gun but she let me go. She was a white lady cop, too. When I saw her I just knew I was going to jail. But it be mostly the black and Puerto Rican cops that mess with you more than the white cops. Most of the time the white cops let you go. Them black cops are the ones that feel they gotta prove something. For real, the black cop feel he have to prove himself to the white cop. The cop be like saying that he gonna let me go this time, and then the black cop say, "No, I think we should take him, no second chance for this one." Just like that. Every single time the police beat me down there was always a black cop or a Puerto Rican. Word.

Last time I got a beat-down I was in Long Island, just for two days. The guy I used to work for was bagging up and I was just playing Nintendo. And the next thing I heard was boom, boom, and they came through the doors—you know, like you see on "COPS"—they was coming through the door. And so my man was throwing all the stuff out the window. I just stayed playing Nintendo. They took the rest of the people out and left me and the two girls, 'cause they found a gun in a box—it wasn't put together, though. So they separated us and put me in one room and hand-cuffed me to one of those chairs that rolls up, you know. I was handcuffed to that and they rolled it up so I didn't have my feet on the ground. Then the DTs came and were asking me whose gun it was and I said, "I don't know." He asked me again and before I could answer he just smacked me, boom! I still had the handcuffs on and I fell on the ground and the cops start kicking me in the stomach, boom, boom, kicking me all in the stomach. That went on for ten minutes, and then I coughed up some blood and that's when they stopped. They took the handcuffs off, shook me around, smacked me a little bit more and said, "Get out of here," and shoved me out the door. Word. Got home all dirty and ripped up and spitting up blood. They took my money. Took my ID. Took everything. My social security, my birth certificate. Had all of that on me. 'Cause when I go to Long Island I carry all of that shit with me so when I hop the train I don't go to jail, I just get a ticket. I didn't get none of that back. They just sent me on my way like that. Had to sit in the bathroom all the way back on the train, didn't have no money to pay for the ticket.

mh: Did you go to the hospital? You were coughing up blood.

tre: Naw, I didn't go to no hospital. My homeboys was laughing at me. They always laughing 'cause I'm always the one who be catching the beat-down. I never be saying nothing. Even when I be getting the beat-down I don't be saying nothing. I don't cry. I don't make no noises, nothing. Be hating it sometimes, though.

mh: Hating what? Hating them or hating the beat-down?

tre: Hatin' life, period. Life. I wonder sometimes, what's the purpose of life? Ain't nothing in my life that went well for me. Word. But if you don't got a crew, then you're lost, I guess. 'Cause everybody else got a crew. If you get into some beef, you gonna need somebody to help you out. Adults be saying you can talk your way out of fights but that's dead. Maybe back in the days. Back when I was twelve or thirteen you could do that. But not now. You can't do that no more. And now I'm eighteen. I used to have a little baby face and everything, and now people say I look older than eighteen. Before, people used to say I used to look younger than sixteen. Done got older overnight. I mean, look at my hands, look at my fingers, slammed in the door, head busted all up. Girl slammed the door on my hand like four times, finger got all messed up. I didn't cry, but I cried when I got my head busted, but I was five or six then. I was with my moms then.

mh: How come you never let yourself cry?

tre: I don't know. It's like I feel like, why waste my time crying over people who don't care nothing about me. The only time I might cry is maybe when one of my brothers die. My mother and father . . . I hate to say that but I don't even know them people. It's just me and my brothers and my sisters. That's it.

Two days later, Tre and I met again. At our first meeting he looked down, gray and depressed. Today, Tre was wearing new jeans, new sneakers, and a big denim coat with huge pockets. He had shaved and left a little mustache and goatee. His eyes were shiny and bright. He looked happy to see me.

We sat in Central Park and talked. Tre told me that after we had our first meeting he went home and ran into some beef. His man, Doo, his best friend from the crew, was jumped by an enemy crew. Doo ran away. Tre found the guys and at first tried talking to them, but then one of them swung on him. They started fighting. The next thing Tre remembered seeing was his friend's hand in front of his face. And then lots of blood.

The kid who was fighting with Tre had pulled out a knife and was going for his face. Doo put his hand over Tre's face and he was stabbed. The fight continued. Some of the other crew ran away when they saw the blood. Tre and his friend jumped the two guys who stayed. A crowd formed, the police came, and they had to pull Tre and Doo off the kids. No one was arrested, and Tre and Doo were taken to the hospital where Doo's hand got more than a dozen stitches.

Tre and I spent close to an hour and a half talking about the fight. He had spent the weekend looking for the crew that did that to his friend. He was gonna flip on them. If he had to, he'd carry his guns (even though he was scared of guns and worried they would shoot off his foot by accident), not to kill them but to shoot them in the foot or the leg and "give them a limp for the rest of their lives." He had all the revenge planned out. Even though Doo had run away from these guys, they had broken the rules and come at him with a knife *without* warning. That's not allowed. I asked Tre whether he thought it was worth it to continue the fight. Who's to say he wouldn't be killed over this? He was the one who had said most of the beefs were about stupid things. But Tre wouldn't budge, at first.

tre: After what they did to me what am I supposed to do now? What am I supposed to do now? I live around there. If I don't do nothin' then every time they see me they gonna be like, "Let's herb him. Take his money and stuff." So I'd rather just get it over with now instead of waiting till later. I'm just gonna send a message to them now. I don't know what I'm gonna do! I just gotta see what happens when I see one of them. I might be in a good mood and might not even say nothing. I don't know. But the way I feel now, if I went home right now and seen them, I'll flip on one of them. Flip on all of them. I was thinking at first that they weren't gonna do nothing, 'cause they never fight me. That's what I was thinking. That it be a quick one-on-one. I thought that was gonna be it. If they didn't stab me in the face then even if I lost or won, I'd be like, "All right, that's cool, check you all later." That would have been it. But I ain't thinking about getting hurt or nothin' like that. I hope I don't get hurt . . . I doubt if I do.

mh: How come you doubt it?

tre: 'Cause I ain't never get hurt. The worst thing that ever happened to me when we got into beef with the crew was I got hit in the knee with a bat. But either I don't ever see these kids again or my man and them squash it without me being around. . . . I don't know. But I don't think my man and them are gonna squash it. They ain't trying to hear that. They thinking the same way as me, that he tried to stab me in the face. I would have rather he tried to stab me in my arm or something. But my face? Come on, man. That's crazy! Talking about them just make me upset. They suckers, the way they did it. That's what make me so upset. They didn't even do it, you know, like he pulls out the knife and I was right there facing it, and then I knew he was coming. He was on that sneak tip, behind me and all. If I'm gonna stab somebody, I ain't gonna just run up behind them and stab 'em. I'm gonna let 'em know. I'm gonna pull it out on them, and then they can do whatever they want to do. I ain't gonna wait till they fighting somebody and then come from behind, sneaking, and try to stab 'em in the face. Word. But then I think about if he did try to stab me in my face, I probably would have been stabbed instead of my man. Now he took the stabbing for me. What am I supposed to tell him? That, naw, I don't want to go get into it no more? Then my crew gonna be thinking, Aw, he soft. He almost got stabbed, now he ain't got no heart. Blah ze blah ze. Yo, but I don't even care what my crew be saying, though. They just got me too mad for that. He shouldn't have did that. Word up. But you asking me all these questions make me think, make me want to change my mind, but . . . what I say now and when I get on the block, it's like totally different, you know?

mh: Where does the violence come from?

tre: I don't know. Maybe that's the nineties. Trademark of my era, I guess . . . Too many movies. I think it's the movies. Word up. I think it's the movies. My man always want to pistol-whip somebody. You remember in *Goodfellas* when he was pistol-whipping and he broke the gun on the guy's face? That's all my man talk about since he seen that movie. "Yo man, I ever catch some kid beefing like that, I'm gonna pistol-whip 'em, break the gun on his face." Word. That's all he talk about since he seen that movie. It be the movies that be making kids do that, act like that. Me? It ain't the movies with me. It's just, I don't know, that's how I was brought up. Been fighting since I was moved away from my moms. Everybody was against me. All the foster homes I went to they used to beat us and everything, till finally I got a little older and I was doing the beating. That's how I felt. Our first foster home, me and my little brother, we used to live with this preacher. He never used to buy us nothing and he wouldn't even feed us. He used to make us eat tomato-and-mayonnaise sandwiches for dinner and everybody else be eating regular food. I used to steal money from him, like two dollars to get me some food to eat. I was so hungry, I took the two dollars and went to school to get me something to eat. So he came to school and he was fronting with the principal like everything was all right and he took me home and he started smacking me all around, like bam, bam, bam, like that. Word. It happened a lot. I was seven, eight, nine years old. I was thinking, yo, I wanted to kill him. If I would've had the heart I got now I would have stabbed that man all up. Back then, I didn't have no heart. I was a little kid. I was just trying to get moved out of that house. And I used to tell the social all about it and she didn't even believe me. This white lady, she didn't believe me. Till finally that time he smacked me all around the face and it was all red and everything, then they moved me out. Then one time my little brother got a big scar on his neck from the ropes the girls be using to jump rope with. The man says that my brother got caught playing with the rope on a tree. But before the man even admitted that happened, he told my little brother, he was like four or five, he told him to tell DSS that I did that to him. They was thinking I tried to kill my little brother. I was breaking down crying, talking to my little brother, telling him to tell the truth. Then finally he went and told that the man did that to him. That's why I don't be having no remorse when I do something like that to somebody. I don't know. When I get mad everything that happened to me come out. You know how you be happy and then all of a sudden it feels like to just boil up, and I get madder and madder and to the point where I just do something. I feel like I be trying to hold it back but then I can't. I can't even explain it, how I feel. It just all boils up. . . . And then I start getting nervous. Like let's say I get mad and if I don't do nothing about it, after a while I just start shaking and get really nervous, my legs and my hands and everything. Until I do something. If I get into a fight then I be all right. After the fight, I'm all calm and cool.

mh: Let me take you back to the movies. It's not what makes you violent, but that's what you think the problem is with other kids?

tre: Yeah, they see that and they want to do that stuff. You know how you be watching karate flicks and you want to go outside and do the same thing they doing? Like when we went to watch *Lethal Weapon 2* and you see that scene when they running around and shooting up stuff. That's what my boys did. They went to this big field and was using dummy bullets and shooting off at each other like they was Rambo or something. I was sitting there, I was drunk, but I was doing a little something myself, I ain't gonna lie.

mh: What's so special about doing that? Makes you feel like you're in the movies?

tre: At that time that's how we felt. Like, yo, we're in the movies, we're gonna do that! Then we be talking like if we ever get into a beef, I'm just gonna grab my two techs, one in each hand and just run through the crowd, shooting. That's how they be thinking. They see a movie and they think they can do it. All those shoot-'em-up bang-bang movies. That stuff be going through their head.

mh: Let me ask you something different. . . . What is it to be a man?

tre: I don't know. Some kids, they have babies and think that makes them a man. Me? What makes you a man is when you take care of your own. When you're on your own and you're doing everything the right way, then you a man. But last year I wanted to have a baby 'cause then I could say to my crew, "Yo man, I got me a kid now. I don't even want to get into that stuff with you." . . . But I can't be having no baby now.

mh: You mean you wanted to have a baby so you could—

tre: Yeah, so I could be like, "Yo, man, I can't be robbing nothing with you all anymore. I got my baby and stuff." I could have used that as an excuse. They'd understand that. But if I just be like, "Naw, I don't want to do it," they'll be like, "What? You got money already?'' And I'll be like, ''No, I'm broke.'' And they'll be like, ''So why you ain't doing it? You scared? What other reason is there? So why you ain't doing it?'' But I'm tired of that. I feel like something gonna happen to me pretty soon if I keep up with that. Everybody going to jail. Everybody in my crew is going to jail or just getting hurt so bad, crippled in a wheelchair or something like that. Ain't none of us ever died. But a couple of us in wheelchairs now. Can't move their back. One of them in a wheelchair now but he starting to learn how to walk. They said he'd never walk again, but he went into that therapy stuff, and he be starting to learn how to walk. But I asking them . . . all of them tell me, ''Yo, man. I felt like this was coming.'' They be telling, ''Yo, man. I felt like I was about to die. I felt like something was gonna happen to me and then this happened.'' They be talking like they knew it was coming. That's how I feel now. They felt it and it happened. And I feel it and I don't want nothin' to happen to me. But I be feeling like I don't want to let 'em down. When I was down and out they looked out for me. I didn't have nobody but them. I didn't even have my mother and father.

mh: You tell them that you love 'em?

tre: Yeah, I tell them. I be like, ''Yo, man, I love you, man.'' Like if something happens or we're about to do something, man, I be like, ''Yo, man, I got bad vibes about this, man. I love you, man. Don't go do it. I'm not doing it, man. Don't go do it.'' Most of the time they listen. If I talk to them like that, and tell them I got a feeling, they won't do it. They be like, "All right—we wait until tomorrow or something."

Tre and I continued to meet over several weeks. I told him I wanted to meet with him and some of the guys from his crew, but with the whole crew there, he said, nobody would be honest. Everybody would be busy putting up a front, dissing each other or dissing me.

Tre's job-training program was almost over and there were no summer jobs for him. He faced getting kicked out of his house if he didn't have a job. He didn't want to go back to selling crack— but he was coming up against a brick wall. There appeared to be no alternative for him. He came to our sessions more angry and more depressed. I asked Tre once how he would like to see the world around him. "Put all the white people in the ghettos and let the blacks live in the suburbs," he said. He would be different then, he said, he wouldn't be so bold.

Over the past year, Tre had helped his boys from the crew if they needed money. He bought them shoes and clothes. But he worried about whether his friends would be there for him when he needed them. The one thing Tre repeated at almost every meeting was how no one in his entire life had ever done anything for him or given him anything for free. He had bought every piece of clothing on his back for himself since he was a kid. Selling crack might be the only thing he knew how to do where he could make decent money. And when he was ready, his crew in Long Island would set him up with a job, in a snap.

mh: How do you feel about selling crack?

tre: It's money. Makin' money, I guess.

mh: You've smoked crack?

tre: Are you crazy! You think I would try to smoke crack? That's an insult. Word up. I ain't tried to smoke no crack. How could you ask me that? Weed and beer be getting me toasted, like I want to go to sleep. So I know I couldn't handle no crack. Baseheads look like zombies. Dirty. They look all sick. They want to smoke it, they gonna get it from somewheres, so I might as well make the money. After this job is over I might end up back in Long Island anyway. I be having bad luck. How am I gonna get money? My moms and pops won't give me nothing. I came up here and tried to stop selling drugs and tried to do me a coupla jobs. But this job stuff ain't working. It ain't even worth it. 'Cause it ain't doing nothing. Even coming to this training program ain't worth it. I coulda made more money just chilling in the street. I'm not gonna ever get no job that I can work at for the rest of my life. I might as well forget it. I ain't fooling nobody. I ain't gonna get no job. I don't got no high school diploma or nothing. I tried this job stuff for a year and it ain't working out. I'm getting kinda old to be broke, not to have a car or my own place or something. This job stuff . . . waiting on a check, waiting on the next check, I hate that. I know after this is over I'm just gonna be sitting there. The only jobs I can get are five dollars an hour in the supermarket and I don't want to do that. I'm eighteen years old. But I'll be paid. I know how to do it. I won't do it how I was doing it before. The way I was doing it before I might get caught. I was selling on the street before.

mh: And now how will you do it?

tre: I'm gonna do it how my man be doing it. I'm just gonna supply people. I'm not gonna be working on the street. I'll buy the stuff, bag it up, and let somebody sell it for me. That's it. I won't sell on the street no more. That's the plan and then hopefully from there I just become big time. That's the only thing I know how to do to make money. That's it. I don't even know how to look for a job. And I'm *not* gonna get a job. I'm *not* gonna get a job. I keep filling out all of these applications and ain't nobody calling me back or nothing. I ain't got no qualifications. And what am I gonna do with a petty job? That's not gonna be enough money for me. I couldn't even pay rent if I wanted to get my own place. Jobs in the supermarket ain't paying nothing. I be broke, just like if I didn't have a job. But it's a shame, though. You know how long I be sitting out here waiting for a job? A good job? And a good job might not even come? No high school diploma, no GED. What kind of job can there be? McDonald's? That's it. But I ain't going on welfare. I ain't gonna be sitting up in no apartment building waiting on no welfare check. I want to get paid. I wish I had a job where I was getting paid. That's what I wish. I wish I had a construction job, to tell you the truth. I'll be all right with that. I be able to handle that.

mh: But have there ever been times, like when you were growing up, when you had dreams about what you wanted to be when you grew up?

tre: I wanted to be an architect. But I got no more dreams. Dreams is dead. I know I can't become it, so why? Shoot. There's nothing I could do. The only thing was to be a basketball player and that's dead. You gotta go to school to become all that. Gotta go to college. I don't even got a high school diploma. And I'm not going to college for no job. I might come out of college and still might not be able to get a job. I don't got no money to go to college anyway. I'll take a city job. Working for transit. Driving a bus or something. That's cool. Even though that's a regular ordinary job, but still it pays the rent. I'd be living on my own. I'm tired of living with my moms and pops. She threatens to kick me out anyway. And there's nothing else I can do. I mean, summer job after summer job. Come on now. Couldn't even take no girl out if I wanted to. Word. Nobody can say I didn't try. Maybe I'm just one of the unlucky ones. Maybe they all think I'm a criminal or something. I don't know. I was all into getting a job at first. Now I don't care about it. Shoot. Just tell me where to go to get an interview and I'll do it. But I know I won't get it. I ain't never had no experience in this. I don't know about going out and applying for jobs and all that. No one ever taught me. I guess I know how to talk and dress. But where to go and what to do to get the job? I don't know all that. And it's a white man's world anyway.

I hadn't spoken to Tre for about one week and we were reaching the end of the project for the book. I called him to set up a meeting and the first thing he asked me was why hadn't I called him. I reminded him that I had told him I wouldn't be calling for a few days because I was going out of town. Out of nowhere, Tre said to me he didn't want to see me again. I said, "What?" He said he had nothing more to share with me and what's more, he didn't know why he had told me anything about his life to begin with. He told me to make sure not to use his name and said he didn't want any pictures to accompany his chapter in the book. And then he hung up on me.

About five days later, I went to the construction site where I knew Tre was working. He was hanging around outside. He saw me but pretended not to. But I just stood there for another five minutes until finally he walked over to me. I told Tre that more than anything what was important was that he understand that I wanted to be a friend. That if he ever needed to talk to anyone he could always call me. "I don't have time to be going out to lunch with you! I don't make any money when I sit with you and talk." I just stared at him. "It's nothing against you. You're still cool with me," he said finally. "But I don't have any time and I don't think I have anything more to say to you and I don't need you." He turned around, put on his construction hat, and walked back into the gray dusty storefront they were renovating.

i'm done fighting

I had been trying to hook up with C-Roy
for several weeks before I finally met
him. C-Roy had taken part in a program to
reform gang members called Aggression
Replacement Training and, at least for now,
he was cutting down on hanging out with
his crew in Brooklyn. The crew has been

around for many years. It's called the Avenue U Boys. For a couple of years C-Roy had been one of the boys.

C-Roy lives far out in Brooklyn, an hour and a half from Manhattan. When I met him the first day, C-Roy was with his girl Shorty. He wanted her to be a part of the interview, just like she was now a part of his life.

C-Roy was wearing baggy shorts down to his knees and a loose T-shirt a couple of sizes too big for his small frame. He had his baseball cap on sideways and was chewing gum and smoking Newports, one right after another. He was nervous, shy, or cocky depending on the questions I was asking. And he didn't talk a lot.

Things were looking up for C-Roy. His dreams were running his life now. He was working with his mother, who owned a used-car lot, and he was getting trained in mechanics. He wanted a straight life—simple, with no cops. But the street never stopped tugging at him. It was his dreams versus the street. His dreams versus his crew. And the struggle continues.

c-roy: We are the Avenue U Boys. All the kids are just friends and hang out on corners and chill. Some people drink beers. A TV reporter called us a gang, but to me it's not a gang. It's all the kids in the neighborhood that I grew up with. To me it was just natural. But then I decided the kids were getting crazy. Recently they just hit a guy in the corner store. Hit him in the face with a bottle, busted his face open. Hit him with a garbage can 'cause the guy wouldn't sell them beer. They do stupid things sometimes. So I decided it was time for me to grow up, and I figured, let me stop hanging out and start doing something with my life. I'm not going to school so I might as well get a job. My mother has a business. So I am working with her, learning the field, and I'll have a substantial job when I get older. I can have a house someday maybe. 'Cause I know a lot of my friends, they're older, they're nineteen, twenty, and some of them are still hanging out.

shorty: They're still selling drugs and they're twenty years old.

c-roy: And I don't be hanging out doing that. I mean, I hang out with my boys and I chill and go out to clubs and raves and stuff, but chilling on the corner, that's not me. I used to drink and I still drink but I'd rather drink at my house or somewheres where I know I'm not gonna get into any trouble. My girl doesn't know, but the reason I stopped hanging out was because of her. Whether she knows it or not.

shorty: Yeah, 'cause these kids get arrested every night. No exaggeration. And every time he stays with them, the cops chase them.

c-roy: It's my block. I hang out in all the buildings and drink beer around there. This one time I went into a building and the door locked and got jammed, and we couldn't get out and so we were kicking the door and it wouldn't open. So this other friend of ours walked by and we told him to kick the door open, and then a guy from the building came out and started chasing us, and the cops came and were chasing us. And then the guy said if he ever saw us in the building again that we were gonna get shot. Then the cops came by and I ran with my friends. So now I gotta worry if I hang out if that guy comes out or if the cops are around 'cause that's my block right there. I don't want any more headaches. Before, I used to live with my father upstate. He used to hit me and beat me. I had a great life up there except for my father. We had a horse ranch. We had acres of field and forest, I had a barn, a dog, and everything. I moved down here and I guess I had to adapt, so I started hanging out with the kids around my house and the neighborhood. I guess that's how I started hanging out with them. My personality comes from Brooklyn now, I guess. I was younger when I came here and I adapted to the city. I like it better than upstate. Here I feel free. I don't have my father straining on me. He was crazy! I had to eat when he eats. The laundry's not done right, the socks are inside out, for everything he was hitting me. He didn't drink. He was an alcohol and drug abuse counselor. He would just swing at me out of the blue when he got mad. The first person I ever fought was my father. He would hit me and I would try to hit him back, and I would get hit even more. It didn't work. So I decided to stay with my mother in Brooklyn. I called up a number my sister gave me, a child abuse hot line, and then we got a court date. We went to family court and my father didn't show up. The third court date he sent a letter saying he felt that I would be better off with my mother, and so right there they gave custody to my mother. I knew he wasn't gonna show up 'cause if he did there would have been this big thing. My mother told me he wasn't gonna show up. I was like, "Yeah he is, yeah he is." Then I started thinking, Why is he gonna show up for? And he didn't. Then I came down here and met the Avenue U Boys and now I got a girlfriend who keeps me straight.

mh: What do your friends think?

c-roy: They always asking me, "Why you with your girlfriend now?" They say, "You're whipped, you're whipped." That's like I'm addicted to her or something, but I am. I'm not whipped, but I like being with my girlfriend, but I also like being with my friends. Now I hang with some guys who weren't part of the crew.

mh: So what's the difference between someone who hangs out with the crew and someone who doesn't?

c-roy: If I was ever walking down the street and I see one of my boys getting beat up I'd be in there. That's my friend. I have to help him. But when they say yo, we're going to fight this crew or that, I'm like, I ain't with it. I'm not gonna go look for trouble, but if it comes to me, I'm gonna deal with it. I don't know what they think. Hopefully they know I'm not a sucker, 'cause I'm not.

mh: Who's a sucker in your mind?

c-roy: Somebody who's scared to go out and fight. But they know that I'm not 'cause I've fought a coupla times and I've prevailed. Like a few months ago, I was with my boys at the movie theater and they were drinking Bacardi, and one of my friends had beef with this girl who was sitting next to us and her boyfriend was sitting there with nine other friends. They started yelling and screaming at each other in the movie. They all were looking at me, but I just kept my mouth shut. We went outside and then my friend was drunk so he fell in a puddle, and then the other kids figured since we were drunk they could beat us up. But I wasn't. So the guy pulled out brass knuckles and he punched my friend in the face, and so I went over there and I hit him. I had to fight four kids. My friend was getting choked and then another friend got arrested 'cause he snapped out. He like went crazy after he got jumped and so he jumped through a car windshield. He kicked it in 'cause he was mad. He had to pay for the windshield. But I've never done really bad things. I've fought people and chased people, but I've never kicked in a car windshield. Never done anything crazy. I don't like to fight but if I have to fight I will. I'm not stupid. I'm not gonna fight with somebody six foot five that starts with me. I go the other way. But if I had to I would pick up a stick or something. I figure if I fight I'm probably gonna get a lot of beatings 'cause I'm smaller than most of my friends. And I have fought my friends before but I don't like fighting my friends.

mh: Why would you have to fight some of your friends?

c-roy: You know, rumors get around about what you say about friends when you're in an argument or something. I told my friend, "If you're gonna hit me, hit me. I'm not gonna hit you back." And I let my friend beat me up right in front of Avenue U. He beat me up. Then I said, "OK, you done hitting me? Good, 'cause now we're gonna find out the truth." And then I found the kid who had lied to my friend about what I had said and I punched him 'cause he lied about me. He said I called my friend a dirty spic. I wouldn't do that. If I did then I would have been wrong for hitting him, but I didn't call my friend that so I felt I kinda had a right to.

shorty: I don't like his friends. They're bad. That's all I have to say.

c-roy: All of my friends?

shorty: Yeah, they are. A lot of them and what they do. I'm just saying. I could never hit my best friend, and if I did then we weren't meant to be friends. So how can you be friends with them after that?

c-roy: I don't know. I guess it's a boy thing. Boys fight, they all fight. I fought. But I'm done fighting. I don't want to fight. I want to work. Make money. Do something with my life. That's another reason I stopped hanging out. 'Cause I lost respect for my crew in a way. 'Cause I was at her grandmother's wake and my friends ran by the place, they knew I was there, and they ran by screaming

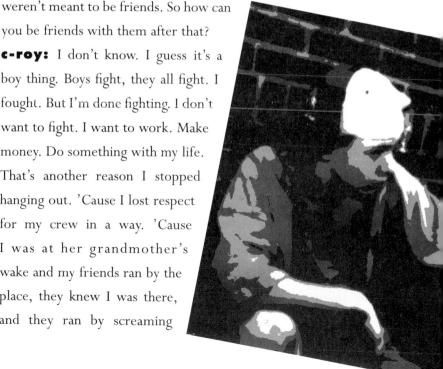

my name. "C-Roy!" I was sitting right next to Shorty's mother. That's no respect.

shorty: In a crew everybody wants a part of the action. Everybody wants to be able to say, "Yeah, I caught this guy," or "I helped my boy, I helped my friends." You get more recognition for that and that's what gangs do. They want recognition. That's why they try to get themselves in the paper. And they do all that stupid stuff to get in the paper to be known as Avenue U Boys. You know, AUB, AUB! And Kings Highway. Stupid gangs. Just so they get known by people. They do nothing with their lives but try to gain fame.

c-roy: Yeah, who's got more fame. Who's tougher. And who would win if we actually had to fight all of you, who would win? It's like that. In a way, it's about territory.

mh: So how many crews are there around here?

c-roy: You got like thirty. You've got Avenue U, Bedford Park, West Kings Highway, East Kings Highway, 52 Park, West Avenue U, East Avenue U, 28th Avenue. But a lot of us are chill with each other. We get along. But sometimes there's beef and we don't get along. One of my friends got stomped out by some kids from Kings Highway. They stomped on his face and beat him up. Hit him with bats. Some kids in the neighborhood can fight. Some kids are tough. But other kids do it just 'cause they like to abuse people.

shorty: Some people will be like, yeah, I'm this or that, but when it comes down to fighting, they need their friends in order to fight. Some people don't fight. They want their crew to fight for them. And the crew will have to do it for them.

mh: You mean, people set people up and get their crew to fight for them?

c-roy: Yeah, like let's say I fight this kid and he beats me up. Of course I would be embarrassed. So then I go and get my boys and say, "Yo, we're gonna beat this kid up and his friends, 'cause him and two of his friends beat me up." So then I call my boys.

shorty: But C-Roy has more respect for people than his friends do. He wouldn't just hit anybody walking down the street. And if his friends were gonna do something stupid he would stop them.

c-roy: I would talk them out of it. I'd be like, "What you gonna do that for?" It don't make me look like a pussy 'cause my friends know if I have to fight I can fight. But they know how I think. I think differently than all my friends. Certain things you can do and then there are certain things where you gotta say, "Yo, what are you doing? Chill!" They try to be tough maybe. They used to go around and beat up the girls on Avenue U, hit them and stuff—

shorty: They abuse girls. Those kids.

c-roy: They spit in your hair, spit in your face. I said to my boys, "Why you doing that?" They diss on the girls and make fun of them. They call them fat and disgusting. They get drunk and pull their hair. I don't know why they do it.

shorty: 'Cause they know they have power over the girls if they do that.

mh: What do the girls say about it?

shorty: If a girl gets abused she won't tell anybody. She'll just look at that guy and say he's a dick, he's a jerk. She won't go into full detail, though, about what he said to her. She just calls him an ass.

c-roy: That is their crew, though. Those are their crew members. That's who they hang out with. They're the girls from the neighborhood who hang out with the guys.

shorty: They consider themselves Avenue U Girls and so they stay with Avenue U Boys. As long as they're with a gang and they know they're popular, they'll get abused or whatever, they don't care. I wasn't down with one crew, I was down with a lot of crews. I was all over the place. I know what they do, and I just don't want to be around it. The minute they started beating people up I'd leave. I mean, I would fight but not like what they would do. They go crazy.

One time I met C-Roy at the subway out by his house. He met me with two of his boys from Avenue U. One guy was a Korean American, the other guy was half-white, half–African American. Both of them had done a lot of the wilding in the crew and they were proud of it. When they did their wilding they were high on drugs. Then nothing mattered—it didn't matter who got hurt. Even if it was yourself. Even if it meant spending the night in jail.

We talked for a few minutes but they had a hard time concentrating or sitting still. After about fifteen minutes of talking with me, they just got up and left me and C-Roy sitting there in the park. These guys were still doing all of the things C-Roy was leaving behind; just by having them around C-Roy felt closer to the tougher guys in the crew. That way he wouldn't lose all his street fame.

C-Roy always had puffy eyes. It looked like he was never getting enough sleep. That was probably because he was at the raves in Manhattan as often as he could be. Raves are where hundreds of kids come together and dance, in peace. Dancing all of the newest steps all night long. It's a safe place most of the time. And since he wasn't out with his boys much, the raves were replacing his crews. The safe crowds of the raves replaced his friends.

mh: What attracted you to your crew?

c-roy: I guess I was attracted to them 'cause they were like me. Wild kids—want to have fun—you know how there are some kids who like after school, they'll go home and do their homework and be good boys, and there are other kids who go home, eat, and then go out and hang out with their friends, instead of being in their house after school? They play sports and stuff, but it's different. They're not like good, normal, everyday boys. I didn't want to be a good little boy. When I lived with my father I couldn't do anything. I wasn't allowed to do anything. I came to Brooklyn and I was just with my mother. And I figured, Well, I can have fun. And so I went out, hung out, got in trouble, started trouble. I would always tell my mom I wasn't gonna get in trouble. And so she would say she trusted me. It just seems like every time I hang out I get in trouble. And I don't like being in trouble. I got to keep my record clean. If I ever want to get a good job when I'm older, I don't want to have things on my record. Arrests and warrants and stuff like that. But we used to have fun play-fighting and joking. Just riffin' on each other, gettin' under each other's skin. It's a contest to see who could last longer and do more dissin' to make the other person feel bad. But it's all in fun. I can make fun of you

'cause you're my boy. But if anyone else says something like that to me and it wasn't my friend, then my boys would jump in and help me. Shorty thinks it's abusing. She and her girls call each other bitches and we riff on each other. Like I got a friend who's chubby. So we say to him, "You and your fat pudge belly butterball-looking self get over here." And you just say stuff like that back and forth for hours. "Your mother eats car bumpers. Your mother is so fat she fell over and broke her leg and gravy poured out." But we don't let it get serious 'cause then we have to get up and start swinging. But we just do it for fun. We go on for a long time.

shorty: I don't see any fun in them abusing each other.

c-roy: It's like to get under each other's skins. In a way it's like helping each other. Like they'll make fun of me 'cause I have some zits. So by them doing that they think it will make me want to make myself look better. By me riffin' on my boy's stomach, maybe it's me telling him he could look better if he worked out a little bit. It's just our own little way of telling each other things. We're not like girls where we'll come up to each other and talk and tell each other straight out. Guys aren't like that. They have to beat around the bush. They don't want to look so obvious. But I've seen my friends fight with people in stores, for real. They went into Dunkin' Donuts and fought with the guy in there and the guy came out with a stick, and they beat him up 'cause the guy pulled a stick on them. If the guy didn't pull the stick on them he wouldn't have gotten beat up. People don't understand us. But you gotta talk to us. We're just like anyone else. You just gotta talk to us. Like about graffiti. Graffiti is big here and getting bigger. A lot of kids from the neighborhood, they try to get fame. They write on walls and say they're up more than anyone else and that they got more fame 'cause more people have seen their name.

shorty: Then you go around and diss other people, crossing their names out and stuff.

c-roy: And then when you meet up with them then you fight it out. Even if I break up with Shorty and sometime in the future I see her brother getting beat up by another crew, I'll step in 'cause he's still my boy. Even though I ain't on the street corners no more I'll fight if I have to.

shorty: A lot of kids don't want to be down with crews. They might be weak and stuff. They have no self-confidence. They don't want to hang out with a gang 'cause then they have to hide behind all their friends. If you're weak, they don't want you to be part of a crew.

c-roy: They call you a herb. If you get into a fight and you run, then you're a sucker. But I don't fight unless I have to fight. I don't go out and start with kids. Some of my friends are like that. But not me. You can't let fear run your life. I've been afraid all my life from my father. He used to hit me. So I figure I'm not ever gonna let anybody hit me again. I'm not gonna get hit no more. I was hit all my life. Nobody's gonna hit me. Somebody hits me, I'm gonna hit them right back. I fought my father. I tried to hit him back and

I got hit worse. If somebody hits me, my first reaction is that I'm scared. But then I think about my father hitting me, and it's like, naw, that ain't happening to me again, not again, no way, no way! And something snaps. I might be small, but I'll pick up anything. I'll use anything to beat somebody up if they try to hit me. No matter how big the kid is. My father used to beat me with everything—with sticks. I felt like I wanted to kill him. Once I pulled a rifle on him. He didn't see me, but I had a rifle behind his back. And I was like, no, I can't do that. And I didn't do that. He didn't even know I had the rifle. I could have put a hole right in him. But I figured, why should I do that? He's my father. He used to hit me with canes, sticks. Over stupid things. He would ask me math questions and math was my hardest subject. I'd be like, "I can't figure out the answer." So he'd get mad and he'd hit me. And he'd hit me 'cause my room wasn't clean. Hit me, like, pow, pow, pow, pow, pow, pow! Until he wanted to stop. I try to push him away and he'd be like, "Don't raise your hands to me!" Pow! I had marks. When I'm in a fight or something, I try to take the pain and turn it into anger and use it. Reverse it. I get hit, so I go right back and hit them back as fast as I can and try not to think about the pain. 'Cause if I think about the pain then I'm just gonna be hurt. And I don't like being hurt.

mh: It happened a lot with your father?

c-roy: Every day. Every other day. I remember once he gave me a beating 'cause I did the laundry and the socks were inside out.

That was the stupidest beating I ever got. Once he found some report cards I had hidden. He called me when I was visiting my mother and he said I had to clean my room. But my room was clean before I left. When I got back my room was ransacked. Closets were knocked over, the bed was flipped up, my dresser was on the floor, clothes were all over the place. That same day I wound up getting hit by a truck. I was riding a bike and I went to hit the brakes and the chain popped and my shoelace got caught and I went straight out in the street. A truck came around and, pow! And I busted my head. I should have gotten money for that but I think my father loused up the case. After I got hit by the truck, two days after I got out of the hospital, he had me stacking wood. I was walking on a cane and he had me stacking piles of wood. I guess he figured I was all right since I was walking around. And I recently got a card from my father, a birthday card, no money, just a phone number. He moved to Florida.

mh: So all the time this was going on what was going on inside you?

c-roy: I wanted to kill him! I felt like a pussy. I was scared. Like a feeling that he hurts me but I can't do anything. And I go in my room and I'd punch the walls and that was all I could do. I couldn't hit him. I was too small. . . . Now, the way I am now, yo, if I was to see my father and he tried to hit me, I would destroy him. I might be small, but I would destroy him. Literally. I'd punch him dead in the nose. With all my might. Break his nose. I'd kick him and drop him to the floor and start stomping on his face. Aaarrghh! But then again, it's feelings like he's my father and I don't want to hurt him, and it's over with and maybe if I did see him again he might be different. But there's always that chance that if he does hit me again, I'm gonna hurt him. I guess I had good times with him, too. You know the thing he's most afraid of is snakes. I'm thinking of mailing him a box full of snakes, big fat ones. Or maybe someday when I have a car, I'll drive there and drop it off, and then I ring the bell and wait behind the bushes and watch him turn white and I'll laugh. If I could scare him the way he put fear into me, then he'll know what I went through. It was the scariest situation you could ever be in. Being scared so much, beaten so much that I didn't know if I was gonna die. Not knowing that if he hit me anymore if he was gonna break something in my body. Not knowing how bad he was gonna hurt me.

mh: So what would a dream family be like?

One that you would feel good about?

c-roy: Like parents that understand what their kids are doing. Like that have gone through it. Like a father that could say, OK, cool, stay out till this time, but call me and let me know what you are doing and where you are and that when I wake up in the morning, you are home. And a father that if you come home and you're all pissed off he won't ignore you. He'd sit down with you and say, "I don't care what happened, I won't get angry, but tell me about it. I'll still love you."

National Public Radio®   New York Bureau   212.878.1430 Tel
801 Second Ave. #701
New York, NY 10017

"ALL THINGS CONSIDERED"

AIR DATE: Tuesday, November 6, 1990

On September 2nd on a New York City subway
platform, one eighteen-year-old stabbed and
killed another. The victim was Brian Watkins,
a tourist from Utah, who was trying to defend
his mother from a mugger. The one charged
with the killing is named Gary Morales. He is
known on the streets of Queens as Rocstar, a
member of the gang called FTS, or Flushing's
Top Society. The headlines about this murder
reawakened fears of the violence carried out
by youth gangs on the streets of New York. We
sent NPR®'s Maria Hinojosa to talk with members of FTS and other Latin gangs, and she
filed this report.

Maria Hinojosa reporting:

Every day after school in the playgrounds of
Junior High School 189 or Public School 40,
members of the gangs from here in Queens hang
out. They spend their afternoons playing
handball, flirting with girls, listening to
music, or painting their graffiti name tags.
The kids who hang out here don't call themselves gang members; they call themselves
posses or crews. These groups are more loose-

knit than a traditional gang. There are no
real hierarchies or defined loyalties, and
the neighborhood isn't a traditional gang
community either. Flushing is a middle-class
area with neat rows of single-family homes
and small condominium apartment buildings.
The kids I meet this warm autumn afternoon
are all affiliated with two crews in the
neighborhood--a crew called 20 Park and
another one known as FTS.

Coki: This is original FTS, right? It started
out in this--in this school right here. It
started out as HBO--Home Boys Only--then
turned into FTS, all right? It stands for
Flushing's Top Society. We fight to survive.
FTS was more like a--go-out, hang-out--hang
out with the guys. That's what it was about.
But, I mean, it wasn't about no--no violence.
But once in a while, you know--once in a
while you do have to defend yourself.

Hinojosa: Coki is a seventeen-year-old Ecuadorian immigrant who's been in the United
States ten years. He's a founding member of
the crew FTS, and like its other members,
he's a relatively recent immigrant from South
America. Coki has just gotten out of school,
and he's lighting up a cigarette, a Newport.
He has on his backpack and is wearing a
hooded sweatshirt pulled up over his head, so
I have to strain to see his face. Once I get
a glimpse of him, though, I see he doesn't
have the look of the hardened street kid.

He's coy, with a baby face and a cute smirk
that comes across every now and then.

Coki: Right now I'm wh--I'm what is known as
an intelligent hood, all right? So . . .

Hinojosa: What do you mean?

Coki: I mean, I go to school. I just--I
dropped out of school, but I realized a lot
of things, I went back. I want my diploma;
it's going to mean something. I'm going to
need it in the future, OK? But I'm trying to
do something with myself, but at the same
time no one's ever going to step on me.

Hinojosa: Coki is a good friend of Rocstar's,
the kid who's now in jail for allegedly
stabbing and killing Brian Watkins, the Utah
tourist. Coki says Rocstar didn't mean to
do it. It was a mistake. Charge him for the
robbery but drop the murder rap, he says. He
looks over to a graffiti memorial he helped
paint on this side of the schoolyard. In a
rainbow of colors, it says, For Brian, In
memory. I asked Coki whether or not Rocstar's
arrest has had an impact on him. He says yes,
but he can't spend all of his time worrying
about what might happen in the future. "I
have to live for today," he says.

About a week later, I had plans to meet the
crew on a Friday night to join them for a
graffiti tagging session. A tag is when you
leave your mark on a wall, a school, a

building, or a subway. Coki is about an hour late. I'm getting ready to leave when I see him and a group of about seven friends walking down this street with a gait, an attitude that smacked of a toughness I hadn't seen before. Coki is giddy, nervously excited; so are his friends. I don't understand until finally Shank, another crew member, tells me they've just been released from a police lineup.

Shank: We were supposed to get picked out if we did the assault, but luckily the guy didn't see who did it so we got off scot-free.

Hinojosa: Wait a second. So does that mean you guys did it?

Shank: Yeah. I mean, we're telling the truth right here. I mean, I don't have nothing to-- as long as my face ain't in there, I'll tell you the truth.

Hinojosa: No, that's not . . .

I became a little nervous as Shank went on to describe what happened the night they decided to, in his words, get paid. Getting paid is the street term for acquiring money or goods. He says they saw a guy looking vic, which in crew language means victim. They decided to go on a mission, which means to assault someone, and then they jumped him. They got enough money for a weekend at the movies and some food.

Shank: He's--he's high, too, don't mind him.

Hinojosa: What are they high on?

Shank: Huh?

Hinojosa: What is he high on?

Shank: Beer or weed or--I don't know. I don't--personally I don't do drugs, but . . .

Hinojosa: But you do assault people?

Shank: Yeah, like they're good at doing drugs; I'm good at this. I get my anger out doing that. You know, see.

Hinojosa: Shank talks about this violence openly, in the same tone he might use to talk about school or a baseball game. I'm taken aback at first, but as Shank continues to describe how he feels and why he does what he does, I realize he understands it quite well. He's angry about his own family violence, angry about seeing too few realistic opportunities for his future, and angry at himself for not being strong enough to give up his habit of assault as a means for relieving his tension.

Shank: I've tried, believe me, I've tried hard. I tried--How do you say it?--constructive things, but I don't know. It just don't give me the same feel of release.

Hinojosa: Well, what do you feel? What do you feel?

Shank: Feel like, you know--you feel, "Ahh,"

you know, like that. That's the only thing I
can do to express it, "Ahh." Like when you
fill up a balloon and it's about to pop and
then you just let the air go, you know,
without letting it pop. You just go "Sss"
and that's it. And then it all builds up
again. It's like a little cycle and stuff.

Hinojosa: And the cycle goes something like
this. The weekend comes around; no one has
any money. Shank has built up little pieces
of anger throughout the whole week, and the
crew decides they want to get paid. Coki, who
I've been told is high on a tab of mescaline,
has joined us now. I ask him why he did this.
"When your father, who's a cab driver now,
was a kid, he would have never thought about
jumping someone to get paid," I tell him.

Coki: The difference between now and thirty
years ago, times are hard now. Believe me,
times are hard. You got no bread on your
table, and your parents can't hack it. You've
got to do something about it; that's your
family and that comes first.

Hinojosa: These kids seem to fit the standard
profile sociologists give to explain youth
violence--kids who start out believing they
can make money legitimately and then lose
hope as they see their own parents' poverty
after years of hard work or, like all other
teens, they are kids who are going through a
stage where they must test their limits. And
there are those who come from broken homes
where there is a history of family violence.

Other sociologists talk about the degree of
violence kids are exposed to in movies or
on TV. But more and more sociologists are
bringing up another form of violence that
doesn't receive as much attention but that is
just as important: the violence of unemploy-
ment, the violence of a poor education, the
violence of racism.

Underneath the Triboro Bridge in Queens,
there is a park with an incomparable view of
Manhattan. Late at night teenagers from all
over the city converge here, and just like
in the 1950s, they spend the night cruising,
driving up and down the road for hours as
they scope out the scene. Coki and Shank told
me to meet them here this Friday night. They
say this park is a neutral zone. Crews from
all over show up, but there is an unspoken
law that no one fights here. This place is
beautiful, with its majestic view of the city
and the river. It's a safe place they use as
an escape from their neighborhoods and the
violence. This evening Coki seems tired, not
of anything in particular, just tired. He
says even though he may feel safe here, there
are bigger problems he can't escape from.

Coki: I think the scariest thing for a teen-
ager is being seventeen years old and being
scared that your parents have no money for
the rent and that you're going to get kicked
out of the house soon and you ain't got nowhere to go, because you ain't got no family
around. I think that's the scariest thing
ever in my life. I've been shot at, I've been

swung at, I've been everything, I--I've done
the same things, but I think that was the
scariest thing. That was it.

Hinojosa: Does being in a crew make you feel
any better? Does it feel--I mean, when you
were there and you did . . .

Coki: Well, it makes you feel powerful. When
you have a name in the street, it makes you
feel fa--makes you feel powerful, OK? You
know, you--I mean, you can't--you're not
powerful in the government because you're not
there. We're the justice in the street. This
is--we're the law, OK?

Hinojosa: The next Saturday night I joined up
with Shank and Coki back in their neighborhood. The crew is getting ready to graffiti-
tag a building with their spray cans. They
paint complex lines that overlap, unreadable
unless you've been initiated into the graf
alphabet. Everyone here has a tag--Gasa, IQ,
Shank, Such One, Zombie, Phantom. It's called
wild style usually, but if you're an expert
writer, it's called cold crush wild style.
Only pros can read those tags. The crews say
graffiti is a way of getting fame. Coki says
it's a way of marking your territory. Ever
since the first youth gangs appeared in New
York City in 1826, territory has always been
key.

Coki: You've got to protect--you've got to
protect what's yours. You've got to protect

your neighborhood, OK? Would you like somebody coming into your house, taking what's
yours, laying back in your couch like--like
it's his--like it's theirs, whatever? You
don't like that, right? OK, same thing, this
is my house. I mean, when you see rich people
a block away and you look at your block and
it looks awful, I mean, it's just--it's just
not right. I mean, why--we're all from the
same place; why must they be better than us?
And we--and that--that's when everything
starts. You're not better than us. We have
to show you you're not better than us.

Shank: Believe me, I know I'm smart. It
sounds really stupid that I see like a big
white man--a big white man, yeah, like about
twenty-five, and I go up to him and I like--
I fight and I beat him up even if--whatever
means I have to do to use it. I beat him up,
and I can look and say see--I said to him,
"At least I'm better than you at something,
even if it's this." I know it sounds real
stupid, but it's still, you know, I do something better than you can. What else can you
do? I mean . . .

Hinojosa: I don't know, what else can you do?

Shank: Huh?

Hinojosa: I mean, you could--you could not do
that, right?

Shank: I could not do that, but then again, I
don't know. Maybe it's the way you're brought

up in this kind of environment--I don't know. As soon as I came here, pow, in a gang like that.

Hinojosa: Shank is interrupted by another crew member who, from a few feet away, calls out, "Five-oh, five-oh," a code for the police. They hide their cans and start to disperse.

Shank: When they say, "Cops," you jump and you run. It's going to get more hectic around here.

Hinojosa: OK, I'm going to go home.

Shank and Coki let me know it would be better if I left. They were afraid some other crew would come around and bring some guns. As I get ready to leave and they're escorting me to the subway so I'll be safe, I ask them why I should feel safe around them, considering what they've done to others. Shank looks at me and says, "We respect you because you showed us respect. We don't like people who are afraid of us. We're not that bad. We just want recognition."

This is Maria Hinojosa reporting.

afterword

Many of the young people I interviewed for this book seemed to believe that where they were when I spoke to them was where they were going to be for a long time. The time that we spent together was one of the few chances they had for self-reflection, a time to look at their lives in a space that felt safe. Everybody grew as a result. And everybody changed.

Shank's life came almost full circle. He has started going to community college and meeting new people. He got a job as a receptionist in a fancy office. A friend got him the interview, but he was hired because he showed that he could do the job. He has had to tone down the "street" in his lingo to answer the phone, but so what? Now he's bilingual. And he's getting paid. Instead of the red rage he used to feel inside, he now says he feels pink. He wishes he could take all of his crew along with him for this new ride. But he's realizing that he can't and that letting go of things just means you learn to trust yourself more.

I didn't talk to Coki for almost a year, but I saw him not too long ago, looking sadder than I had ever seen him. He had been going to school to learn air-conditioning repair, but he dropped out when his teacher started doing drugs with him after class. Coki always talked like he thought he could do something with his life. Now it seems he doesn't have that hope. He used to take his pain out doing missions with the crew. Now that pain is just eating him up. But he is so worried about what everybody thinks of him that he can't take the first step to look for help.

IQ lost his son to his ex-wife in a custody battle. His boy was the one thing that kept IQ going. He was committed to raising his son in a different way than he had been raised. Now that his boy is gone, IQ says it feels like something inside him has died. He's working in the mail room of a big company. He still hangs out in the park, and the younger crews still look up to him. He wants to be a role model for his son, but he still likes to be on the street; the big question for him is how to do both.

Smooth B and Sonya had little baby boys. Sonya's boyfriend has actually stuck around to be a father to his child. Smooth B wants to go back to school. She wants to get a job. But with a baby, everything seems difficult. Most of the GICs don't hang that much anymore. As they get older, more responsibilities set in: babies, the possibility of college, jobs. It seems, also, that the GICs have started to look to men for the support they once found in each other.

Tre has never contacted me, and although I've called him, he's never returned my calls.

C-Roy and Shorty broke up after being together for a year and a half. It had to do with drugs. Shorty was upset that C-Roy had started hanging with a crew that was into drugs, and C-Roy chose his friends and his partying over Shorty. The last time we spoke, C-Roy had just gotten a job doing construction work, and he was also getting paid for dancing at raves.

And the new word on the street is that a stint in jail is not such a bad thing. Spending time in jail is one of the newest ways of getting respect.

—Maria Hinojosa
New York, 1994

glossary

BAG UP — package drugs in plastic bags for selling

BASEHEAD — cocaine free-base addict

BEAT-DOWN — beating

BEEF — problem that might be resolved through fighting

BEING DOWN WITH — being a member of, agreeing with

BOP — angel dust

BOPPED UP — high on angel dust

BUGGING OUT — upset, freaking out, high on drugs

BUM RUSH — when several crew members attack one person

CATCH YOUR BACK — watch behind your back

CHILL, CHILLING — act calm, calm down

CRACKHEAD — someone who's addicted to crack

CRILLS — crack

DISSING — criticizing; shortened form of "to disrespect"

DOPE — heroin

DOWN WITH — cool with, in good standing

DUMMIES — fake drugs

FLIP ON SOMEONE — turn against someone suddenly, betray or
    attack someone

FRONTING ON/WITH — pretending, putting up a false front

GETTING CHOPPED — getting high on marijuana

GETTING LARGE — getting recognition; getting money

GETTING PAID — making money in any way possible

GO AWOL — run away

HERB — a weakling, a person who can't stand his or her ground

TO HERB — to attack or jump a weaker person

HOMEBOY/HOMEGIRL — fellow crew member, friend

'HOOD — neighborhood

HOODIE — hooded shirt or jacket

HOP THE TRAIN — ride the subway without paying

MESS SOMEBODY UP — beat somebody up

MY MAN — my friend

ON THE SNEAK TIP — observing secretly

PACK — to carry a weapon

POSSE — a gang or crew

RIFFING ON — making fun of, joking

SLEEPER HOLD — a wrestling-type hold in which you grab some-
        one by the neck and push so they instantly
        pass out
SOCIAL — social worker
STEP TO — get into a fight with someone
SUCKER — somebody who's afraid to fight
TAG — a graffiti writer's street name
TAGGING — writing graffiti on walls
TECHS — a kind of nine-millimeter gun
VIC — victim
WASSUP? — what's up?
WEED — marijuana
WILDING — wandering the streets starting trouble or fights
WORD — expression meaning ''of course, absolutely, that's true''

spanish words and phrases

Aguantando — dealing with it
Cabrona — bitch
Educado — educated
Se le sale como agua. — It pours out like water.
¡Tu eres tan puta! Tu no haces esto, cabrona. ¡Hija de la gran puta! —
You are such a slut! Don't do this, bitch. Daughter of the biggest
slut!
Vaya con Dios. — Go with God.